The Price of Truth

The Price of Truth

*Sermons Preached at
Emerson Unitarian Church*

FRANK SCHULMAN

Meadville Lombard Press
Chicago, Illinois

The Price of Truth
Edited by Mark Edmiston-Lange
Copyright © 2006 by Alice Schulman

First Edition 2006

All rights reserved. No part of this book may be reproduced in any manner without written permission except for quotations embodied in critical articles or reviews. For additional information write to:

Meadville Lombard Press
5701 S. Woodlawn Avenue
Chicago, IL 60637

Cover design, book design, and typesetting by Dan Doolin

ISBN: 0-9702479-8-2
ISBN: 978-0-9702479-8-8

Library of Congress Control Number: 2005938174

Printed in the United States of America

Contents

Foreword *by Mark and Becky Edmiston-Lange*	vii
Introduction	1
The Price of Truth	3
"The Boston Heresy": Unitarianism in America	11
Unitarianism Begins, I: *Servetus*	21
Verdict by the Syndics of Geneva	29
Unitarianism Begins, II: *Castellio*	31
From Concerning Heretics, *by Sebastian Castellio*	40
William Ellery Channing: A *Study in Greatness*	43
From Unitarian Christianity, *by William Ellery Channing*	52
"God Is One!" Four Hundred Years of Unitarianism	55
Act of Religious Tolerance and Freedom of Conscience, *issued by King John Szigismund*	62
Emerson and Compensation	65
Why Pray?	73
Axioms of Theology	81
The Message of Jesus	89
Religious Experience	99
Prayers	107

Foreword
by
Mark and Becky Edmiston-Lange

We had known *about* Frank for years. His scholarship, particularly regarding R. W. Emerson, was widely celebrated. But Frank was not the sort of denominational creature who attended General Assembly, so meeting him in person did not take place until we moved to Houston to take up a co-ministry for the congregation he had served for 25 years. We were lucky to have him as a colleague and friend for the last six years of his life.

First, and the fact of which he was most proud (although he never exhibited pridefulness), he helped build a very strong and deeply committed congregation on the west side of Houston. Furthermore, Frank used his Sundays when not in the pulpit at Emerson (and continuing throughout his "retirement") to travel to neighboring small outposts of Unitarian Universalism to conduct worship. He was an institutionalist, doing all that he could to build strong churches and strong congregations. But his intellectual framework for building a strong church had little to do with Alban Institute research and late-breaking monographs on public relations efforts. Frank's point of view was almost entirely theological. He believed the church existed for one purpose: to save souls from the many forms of perdition that infect human existence. Other people became a part of it for other reasons, e.g. to find a community, to educate children, to protest injustice in the world. Frank wasn't opposed to those motivations, but they were to him byproducts, not the central unifying raison d'être for the church.

Simply put, he loved his faith. He loved its intellectual sturdiness, its bracing honesty, and its enduring loyalty to truth-telling. He could be very focused, and sometimes insistent about his point of view, but always because he loved his faith. He loved the religion of Unitarian Universalism, he loved the history of that religion, and inevitably sought to ground almost any conversation in those enduring passions of his life.

Frank loved tradition and was widely known for resisting modernizing trends that were not, by his lights, an improvement. But few know that in the earliest years of women entering ministry in the modern era, Frank was alone among his colleagues in the Southwest District in supporting women in the ministry, providing an internship for Alice Blair Wesley. Again, it was the faith that was essential. Man or woman—that was not.

Frank was not the least bit calculating in his decision making. He believed that once you came to a belief about the right course of action, you did it. His success at Emerson can be greatly attributed to the fact that he was a very gifted preacher. But the more important factor in his eyes was hard work. From Frank's point of view, ministry was not supposed to be easy. It required sacrifice, sometimes obscenely long and unrewarding hours. The willingness to work for something in which you believed—that was what truly mattered to Frank, and that was how Frank conducted himself.

The church he helped build still stands strong, accustomed to a deep commitment to bracing honesty and wide-ranging thoughtfulness. The following chapters in this book provide only a sample of the wisdom and affection of Jacob Frank Schulman, Frank.

Introduction

Sermons are a special form of communication. They combine thought of the divine with appeal to the rational and devotional sense of the congregation. Sermons vary in their intent: information, inspiration, spur to social action, consolation, or purging wrongs, both in society and by individuals. Sermons aim to enhance faith and hope. They try to make sense out of what often seems senseless, to show that our endeavors are not in vain, and that there is a source beyond us on which we can rely.

Sermons are not intended to be literary works, nor to demonstrate the preacher's learning or wit. They may be prophetic or priestly, designed to disturb, comfort, or challenge. The sermon ought to come from the heart, with the minister as witness of a great tradition. Remember that sermons are intended to be heard in the context of worship, surrounded by hymns, readings, prayers, and anthems. But perhaps they are not devoid of interest standing alone.

This sampling of sermons was delivered at Emerson Unitarian Church during my ministry there, from 1963 to 1988, after which I retired and continued my ministry in England. There I found my way into both academic and pastoral work and concentrated on research that resulted in several books dealing with Unitarian history.

The selection of sermons here avoids topical subjects that may have been important once but now would be only curiosities.

Introduction

Times move quickly. I recall once, during the Vietnam War, I wrote a sermon intended for delivery in two weeks, but by then it was out of date. When I retired I went through my sermons and discarded a large number of them. I discovered that those still worth preaching dealt with doctrine, the Bible, theology, history, biography, and the fundamentals of religion. Some of those are reprinted here.

"The Price of Truth" and "Religious Experience" underscore the philosophy of Unitarianism. Several are theological: "Axioms of Theology," "The Message of Jesus," and "Why Pray?" I limited biography to two, though a great number could have been printed: "William Ellery Channing: A Study in Greatness" and "Emerson and Compensation." There are four that deal with our history. I have noticed over the years a great interest in our history, filled as it is with heroic deeds and people of great stature. "God is One!" tells the exciting story of Francis David and King John Szigismund. Two are devoted to Servetus and Calvin: "Unitarianism Begins: Servetus" and "Unitarianism Begins: Castellio." Finally comes the story of our beginnings in America: "The Boston Heresy."

Appended are some prayers delivered during the worship at Emerson Church. Perhaps they will bring some comfort and ease to the grief and confusion of our times.

—Frank Schulman

The Price of Truth

We talk a lot about the search for truth, and we believe truth can be found everywhere. We see truth in the many religions of the world, in the sciences and the humanities. We find truth in human struggles, in our hopes and dreams and visions.

People sometimes think of Unitarianism as an easy religion, in which one can believe anything, or nothing at all. That is not so. Unitarianism can be casual and thoughtless but it should not be so, because the price of truth is high. And if you want truth, you must pay for it. There are four prices.

I.

The first price of truth is humility. Will Durant said the first rule of philosophy is that we may all be mistaken. To learn, as every wise person knows, we must be humble. We must recognize that our own ability is limited. Seneca had that sense of humility when he said,

> How does one acquire wisdom? By practicing it daily, in however modest a degree; by examining your conduct of each day at its close; by being harsh to your own faults and

lenient to those of others; by associating with those who exceed you in wisdom and virtue; by taking some acknowledged sage as your invisible counselor and judge.

Truth must not be arrogant or rude. William Penn said, "Truth often suffers more by the heat of its defenders than by the argument of its opposers."

We must pay for truth with the price of humility. Where would science be today if those who dissented from the accepted theories had been burned at the stake? Religion too often acted that way and it has suffered because of it. We must search for truth with diligence, and the price we pay is humility. Heinrich Heine described [the philosopher Gotthold] Lessing this way:

> Lessing would not grant the slightest concession to a lie, even though by doing so, after the manner of the wise men of the world, he might promote the triumph of truth. He dared do everything for truth except lie. Whoever, Lessing once said, supposes that he may bring truth to the market under all sorts of artifices and disguises, may indeed be the pander[er], but he has never been the lover, of truth.

A second price we must pay for truth is pain. Giving up long-cherished ideas is not easy. We have an emotional attachment to ideas. Love of parents may prompt us to accept their beliefs. Then when we reject their beliefs we feel guilty, as if we had betrayed them. So rejecting what they stood for may be a way of rejecting our parents. It can work the other way, too. Teenagers and college students who want to find a still better way feel they must first throw off the religion of their parents. That isn't easy. Steve Allen, in his book *The Funny Men*, told the story of a Jewish man who was going to a psychiatrist. He had rejected the religion of his parents and said it was all stuff and nonsense. He was going to the psychiatrist because every time he ate pork he got deathly sick. In the Hottentot culture part of the ritual of entering adulthood is that the young man must beat his mother.

The Price of Truth

Many people want to avoid the pain of searching for truth. It's hard for us to admit that there are subjects about which we aren't decided, or about which we cannot form an adequate opinion. The demand is for people of decision, people of action. Breaking in a new opinion, which means giving up something comfortable, is hard. John Stuart Mill wrote, "There is no philosophy possible, where fear of consequences is a stronger principle than love of truth."

So we resent those who show us we are wrong, like the Athenian idiot who railed against the doctor for curing him of the insane delusion that he was rich. We should hold those who correct us in affection. It is all so painful: to reject things long believed, the comfort of the creeds, the deity of Christ, the virgin birth, heaven and hell, the Bible as literal truth. Giving up such beliefs can be as painful as the extraction of a tooth. Or for Unitarians it may be just as painful to believe in a meaningful God, to admit that there is something greater than us. We speak of tolerance but in some of our churches to call a person a Christian is the moral equivalent of child molesting. All of us have blind spots, and maybe we reject extra-sensory perception, astrology, and flying saucers just because it is too much work, and too painful, to reassess our whole intellectual structure.

II.

To question thoroughly, to seek earnestly, may bring social disgrace. Fred Gladstone Bratton, a church historian, said,

> The irony of history is that unwarranted hostility and insult have always been directed towards men whose only ambition was to find the truth.

Albert Schweitzer found that out, and he was not disturbed. If one seeks truth, he said, one must not expect that others will help roll the stones out of the path. In fact, one must not be surprised if they even roll a few more stones *onto* the path.

The Price of Truth

And so the third price we pay for truth is human opposition. We often are made to feel that we are attacking and interfering with all kinds of vested interests. It makes little difference what area of life we are talking about. There are always those who are offended by a difference of opinion and somehow will translate your good intentions, your honest search after truth, into some label such as anarchist, fascist, secular humanist or something of that sort. That isn't easy. We all want friends and we want to be liked. But if we devote ourselves to the search for truth we must learn early that there is a higher goal than being liked:

> "You have no enemies, you say:
> Alas, my friend, your boast is poor."

Search for truth we must, whatever the consequences. An early motto of the American Unitarian Association was *In luce veritatis:* "In the light of truth." Walter Bagehot wrote, "The whole history of civilization is strewn with creeds and institutions which were invaluable at first, and deadly afterwards."

Schweitzer said, "It is the fate of every truth to be ridiculed before it is accepted." That doesn't mean that every hated idea today will some day be accepted as true, but it does mean that among all the ideas we now sneer at are some that one day will be considered truth. So we must realize that part of the price of truth is human opposition. Ausonius, a fourth-century Roman scholar, laid down the dictum, *Veritas odium parit:* "Truth purchases hatred."

If we will have the truth, we must pay for it. The only really important consideration is whether the price is too high. If the price is too high, we must be willing to settle for something less than truth. It depends in the end on what estimate we have of ourselves. How strong are we? How highly do we value integrity? Do we believe it is worthwhile to be noble? Are we more concerned with popularity, with what the world calls success, or with our own integrity? It is that simple, and that is the price we must pay for truth.

Mark Twain became publisher of *The Buffalo Express*. On the first day he wrote an editorial in which he said, "I shall always confine myself to the truth, except when it is attended with inconvenience." And we all know that is true of us. That "inconvenience," as old Mark called it, must not be taken lightly. Truth is hard. James Russell Lowell said in his poem,

> *Then to side with truth is noble when we share her wretched crust,*
> *Ere her cause bring fame and profit, and 'tis prosperous to be just;*
> *Then it is the brave man chooses while the coward stands aside,*
> *Doubting in his abject spirit, till his Lord is crucified.*

And so we must pay these prices for truth: humility, pain, and human opposition. None of us wants to pay that price, and we might wish the scheme of the universe were different. But there is a divine wisdom behind this, for, as Thomas Paine said, we value lightly what we obtain cheaply, and it would be strange indeed if so prized an object as truth came easily. What progress we have made along these lines has come to us because brave people suffered. Socrates drank hemlock, Jesus was crucified, Servetus was burned at the stake, and Castellio was starved to death. To accept what they gave us and go no further is to betray what they lived and died for. Our job is to push on to more truth.

III.

So, besides the three prices of truth—humility, pain, and human opposition—there is a fourth price to pay: responsibility.

If there is truth, there is also the moral obligation to act according to what we believe to be the truth. It is hard. When we see a street person, someone with AIDS, or any suffering, it is easier to pass by, as the priest and the Levite did, but truth makes its demands. We may feel superior when we despise people because of their skin color or social condition, but we know that is wrong. There are times that prompt us to cruelty, but we know that is wrong, too. We know it is wrong to cheat or lie, but sometimes that seems the best way to get along in the world. Suppose a lie helps a friend when telling the truth would hurt. What do you do then?

But responsibility there is toward truth. Being a citizen implies responsibilities. Being a member of your church carries responsibilities. Being adult has its demands, too. So does being a spouse, employer, or tradesman. The point is that the search for truth is wasted unless we take it seriously. Samuel Johnson said,

> Between falsehood and useless truth, there is little difference. As gold that he cannot spend will make no man rich, so knowledge that he does not apply will make no man wise.

We also must feel a corporate responsibility in our search for truth. The advantage of searching in community, of joining as a church for that purpose, is that we support each other in our struggles. "Prayers travel more strongly when said in unison," wrote Petronius. Alexander Pope said,

> When truth or virtue an affront endures,
> Th' affront is mine, my friend, and should be yours.

IV.

So these are the prices we must pay. I hope we are all searching for truth in our own ways. But these prices of truth apply to churches as well. The church must be willing to endure pain and human opposition, and assume both humility and responsibility for what truth it holds. The church must do things that are not easy. It must suffer the slings and arrows of outraged society. Often to preserve its integrity the church must do the very things that will cause some of its people to turn away in anger. You may have reason to wince at what the church has done, but I hope you never have to question its integrity.

People, people who have fears and doubts, and who want life to be uncomplicated, run churches. And so religion has become easy. It asks little. It blows with every wind, responding always to the majority will instead of making its demands on the basis of what it holds to be right.

Religion is afraid to challenge, afraid to break the idols of popularity. Religion has lost its force in modern times, and we like to blame secular science, or anti-religious philosophy, or the televangelists. It would be more honest to blame ourselves if our religion has lost its influence.

Religion declined, not because it was refuted, but because it became irrelevant, dull, oppressive, and insipid. When faith is replaced by creed, worship by group discussion, and love by habit; when faith becomes an heirloom rather than a living fountain; when religion refuses even to face the fundamental questions of its authority and purpose, its message becomes meaningless.

Don't forget it: the task of religion is to deal with ultimate questions. That's what it really means to be relevant. The church, like people who compose the church, must ever search for truth, and the price exacted is high. Churchill warned that he had nothing to offer but blood, toil, sweat, and tears.

So I warn you. Humility, pain, human opposition, and responsibility: those are the price of truth. The price is high, but there can be no compromise. If you don't want to pay the price, you don't want the truth. That's all there is to it. If you want something else, something more comfortable, go elsewhere. You will not like it here.

The price of truth is high, but it is worth the whole of the struggle. As religious people we do not ask that the way be made easy, only that here we may find the strength and wisdom for the struggle.

"The Boston Heresy"

Unitarianism in America

The founding of Unitarianism in America is an exciting story. There are heroes whom we should admire for their courage. We should know their sacrifice and share their joys while we bear witness to their bravery. At the conclusion I will list four beliefs they held in common, beliefs that bind us into a great family, not only with each other but also with those noble people who founded our religion. We have a history going back over two hundred years in America.

I.

New England until 1755 was entirely in the hands of the Puritans, those stern Calvinists who believed in the depravity of human nature, salvation of the elect, and predestination. They said there was no hope for anyone, that we were all born entirely depraved. In that gloomy climate came the first man in America we may call an outspoken Unitarian. Not many know of him, and his story needs to be celebrated more widely than in the dusty annals of history books.

The man in America we may call the first Unitarian was the Rev. Jonathan Mayhew. He was the son of the Calvinist preacher, Experience Mayhew. What delightful names they had in those days. Jonathan Mayhew was the minister of the West Church in Boston. He was known as a heretic and embraced the Unitarian position. So hated was he that no Boston minister would exchange pulpits with him. He was not invited to join the ministerial association. The clergy shunned him. But his congregation grew. No minister in Boston had nobler, broader, more humane qualities.

Mayhew's main quality was freedom of inquiry. He taught freedom and toleration everywhere. He said,

> How much soever any man may be mistaken in opinion concerning the terms of salvation, yet if he is practically in the right there is no doubt but he will be accepted by God.

No speculative error, he said, will keep a good person out of heaven. Grace is available to all. He preached the essential goodness of human nature. He was a rationalist, a defender of freedom. His sermons were plain, direct, vigorous, and modern. He taught humanitarian religion, genuinely ethical. The important thing in religion, he said, is not doctrines, creeds, or beliefs, but to love God and our neighbor, to have piety of heart, to be righteous and just, holy and charitable. He insisted on the strict unity of God. Jonathan Mayhew said to his congregation,

> There is nothing more foolish and superstitious than a veneration for ancient creeds and doctrines as such, and nothing is more unworthy a reasonable creature than to value principles by their age, as some men do their wines.

By 1786 several Unitarians in Boston gathered to discuss their common theology and how to confront the Calvinists. They were aided by a misfortune across the ocean. In 1787 Joseph Priestley's home and his church in Birmingham, England were burned. Priestley came to this country and founded Unitarian churches. He

"The Boston Heresy"

was a learned and pious man. He attracted many great names to his church in Philadelphia. Regular attendees in his congregation included Thomas Jefferson, Benjamin Franklin, and Thomas Paine.

The movement grew. In 1787 Dr. James Freeman Clarke wrote a friend,

> I cannot express to you the avidity with which the Unitarian publications are sought after. Our friends here are clearly convinced that the Unitarian doctrine will soon become the prevailing opinion in this country. Three years ago I did not know a single Unitarian in this part of the country beside myself; and now . . . a decent society might be collected in this and the neighboring towns.

As the nineteenth-century opened, Unitarianism had grown enough that it represented an ominous threat to the Calvinists. The Calvinists could scarcely contain themselves. The controversy broke into full war in 1805 when the Rev. Henry Ware, Sr. of Hingham was appointed to the Hollis Chair of Divinity at Harvard. He was the first Unitarian to occupy that high place. And then all the faculty of the divinity school became Unitarian, and Calvinists gnashed their teeth. Lyman Beecher, leader of the orthodox, said,

> Unitarianism was fire in my bones. My mind was all the time heating—heating—heating.

He anticipated the day when "victory will be achieved, and Unitarianism cease to darken and pollute the land." That sentiment was shared generally. A Methodist hymn of that time that included these lines:

> *Send down thy wrath, thou triune God,*
> *The Unitarian fiend expel,*
> *And chase his doctrines back to Hell.*[1]

---

[1] "Sun of Unclouded Righteousness"

Unitarianism in all its forms was regarded by the Calvinists as a deadly foe of human happiness whose result, they said, would be to prevent true conviction and conversion, stop revivals, and leave men in the hands of Satan.

Unitarianism was accused of denying the divinity of Christ, the total depravity of man, and the vicarious atonement. The Calvinists said [such views] would stop the work of salvation. Beecher thundered that the Unitarians "with their power of corrupting the youth of the Commonwealth by means of Cambridge"—he meant taking over Harvard—were "silently putting sentinels in all the churches, legislators in the halls, and judges on the bench, a scattering everywhere of physicians, lawyers, and merchants." They "sowed tales while men slept and grafted heretical churches on orthodox stumps."

Unitarians were accused of undermining revealed religion, particularly because they did not believe in human depravity, the Trinity, and the revelation of scriptures. At least they didn't believe in those things as the Calvinists did.

II.

Unitarians went on the offensive and attacked the Calvinists. William Ellery Channing said,

> Unitarianism is Christianity stripped of those corrupt additions that shock reason and our moral feelings. It is a rational system, against which no man's understanding, or conscience, or charity, or piety revolts. Can the same be said of that system which teaches the doctrine of three equal persons in one God, of natural and total depravity, of infinite atonement, of special and electing grace, and of the everlasting misery of the non-elected part of mankind?

It was a war of the pamphlets. Henry Ware, Sr. titled a pamphlet *Letters to Trinitarians and Calvinists*. He said,

> If the doctrine of depravity... cannot be perceived by us to be consistent with the moral perfection of God, then presumption is very strong, that it is not true. Depravity is inconsistent with God's love and justice because it means that mankind is damned without giving them any choice in the matter.

Leonard Woods spoke for the orthodox. The main fight was over the question of total depravity. He wrote,

> That men are by nature destitute of holiness; or that they are objects of an innate moral depravity; or, in other words, that they are from the first inclined to evil, and that, while unrenewed, their moral affections and actions are wholly wrong.

Ware said that position was inconsistent with the moral perfection of God. Man, he argued, as he is born into the world, comes from the hands of God innocent and pure, free from all moral corruption.

> Man is by nature [wrote Ware] no more inclined or disposed to vice than virtue, and is equally capable in the ordinary use of his faculties and with the common assistance afforded him, of either.

Leonard Woods accused Channing of having misstated the Calvinist position. Woods defended the doctrines of total depravity, vicarious atonement, and election. Ugly as they are, he said, they are true. Channing and Ware replied by citing orthodox authorities, including Calvin himself, so clear and definite that they could not be evaded or explained away.

The Unitarians made their appeal to reason, conscience, and human experience. Ezra Styles Gannett, a leading proponent of Unitarianism, said the charges reduced themselves simply to narrow insistence that one must swallow the whole of Calvinism. Francis Greenwood said that Unitarianism simply would not be committed to "a timid creed-bound theology."

III.

So the "Boston Heresy," as it was known, spread rapidly. A radical change was taking place in Boston religion: a great change, and quickly. To turn Calvinism into Unitarianism, to substitute William Ellery Channing for Jonathan Edwards, to see Ralph Waldo Emerson gracefully climbing the pulpit where once Cotton Mather presided, was a rapidly effected change. The orthodox saw Unitarianism as a movement to be expunged.

Then church after church converted to the new religion, all over New England. The famous King's Chapel, the first Anglican Church in this country, took the tenets and the name Unitarian. So did the church of the Pilgrim Fathers in Plymouth. So did hundreds of churches in towns throughout New England.

Unitarians worked for disestablishment. They were against state support of the churches, an idea that was then almost universally accepted. The Unitarians did not want any exclusive rights, as did other denominations when they gained power. The Unitarians wanted only equality.

Unitarians identified with the American Revolution, which had a liberalizing influence on religion. It broke old customs and required religious freedom. In open and free debate the Unitarians were confident, so long as the flames could not be set to dissenters, so long as damp prison cells did not await heretics.

The war of the pamphlets continued. Scholars scratched away in the small hours of the night. John Sherman wrote his pamphlet *One God in One Person*. Hosea Ballou wrote his *Treatise on the Atonement*.

In 1799 William Emerson, father of Ralph Waldo, became minister of the First Church in Boston, the most hallowed and ancient church in that venerable city. In 1803 Channing was called to the Federal Street Church. Channing was a man of profound piety and scholarship. He came to liberalism because of his love of freedom, his lofty spiritual nature, his tolerant cast of mind. He gave spiritual and intellection direction to the movement.

"The Boston Heresy"

Unitarians published widely and they became intellectual leaders of the nation. They founded *The Monthly Anthology, The General Repository and Review, The Christian Register, The Christian Disciple,* and *The Bible News*. They founded many charitable institutions.

The fire was building. In 1815 Dr. Jedediah Morse,[2] a leading Calvinist, accused the heretics of being nothing more than Unitarians. The term "Unitarian" then was one of hatred. It was not accepted by the liberals, who still were Congregationalists. Morse aimed to force them to declare themselves or renounce their heresies. The Unitarians were reluctant, mostly because they did not want to form another sect.

But then the skies darkened and the clouds gathered. From 1815 to 1819 the Unitarians remained on the defensive. Then in May 1819 the full fury of the storm broke. One Jared Sparks was to be ordained in Baltimore. He asked Channing to preach the sermon. Channing took for his text, "Prove all things, hold fast that which is good." That sermon, *Unitarian Christianity*, one of the two most famous sermons ever preached in this country—the other being Emerson's *Divinity School Address*—was a powerful and scholarly attack on the Trinitarian doctrine. Channing called on the Unitarians to embrace the new doctrine.

The response was electric. Church after church followed Channing's lead until finally there was not a church in all Boston that was not Unitarian. So many were they that on May 25, 1825 a group of prominent Unitarian ministers met in Boston to organize themselves into an association. They undertook to provide services and publish tracts for the spread of pure Christianity. There were now 125 Unitarian churches within 25 miles of Boston and a few as far away as New York and Washington.

There were many prominent and beloved men among the leaders, names we ought to remember: Dr. Charles Chauncey, Ebenezer Gay, William Hazlitt, Ezra Styles Gannett, James Freeman, Edward Everett, Henry Ware, and Andrews Norton. Henry Adams wrote of them,

---

[2] He was the father of Samuel F. B. Morse, who became Unitarian.

Nothing quieted doubt so completely as the mental calm of the Unitarian clergy. In uniform excellence of life and character, moral and intellectual, the score of Unitarian clergy, who controlled society and Harvard College, were never excelled.

IV.

This, then, is a brief history of our movement and our heritage. We conclude with a statement of the four doctrines that bound them. These four beliefs held the movement together. It is what we would call normative Unitarianism. These are the beliefs that summoned the consciences and minds of a great people, which fired them with enthusiasm and set the stage for rational religion.

First, the unity of God. "One God in one person" was the motto. There is one God without rival or competition. It is our obligation to imitate the perfection of God, to grow in God's image and likeness.

Second, the innate goodness of all people. Every person is born with a capacity for goodness, which it is the job of the church to enhance. We all are created in God's image. We have one God of all people and we are brothers and sisters to each other. Jesus, too, was our brother, and in him we have an exemplar and teacher.

Third, the appeal to reason in matters of belief. The Unitarians knew their Bible, and they sought inspiration from it. They studied it thoroughly in the light of historical and textual criticism. They opened the study of world religions. They championed the growing knowledge from science and the humanities. But all religious teaching and instruction must appeal to our highest faculty, the intellect.

Fourth, the duty of people to do justice, to take seriously the command to love our neighbor as ourselves. The church is committed to the establishment of the Kingdom of God here on earth. It is within our reach. There is much you and I can do to speed its coming. We have laid on us the moral obligation to virtue, to duty, to responsibility for the common good.

Unitarians stressed all those points. They spoke of salvation by character, not vicarious atonement. They believed in the leadership of Jesus, not recitation of creeds. They talked of the goodness of people, not our total depravity.

Those four beliefs we may take as the legacy delivered to us: first, the unity of God; second, the innate goodness of all people; third, the appeal to reason in matters of belief; and, fourth, the obligation of duty and moral responsibility.

That is the heritage of those great and valiant people who suffered so, who gave up honor and fortune that we might worship in freedom, in spirit, and in truth. That is what is meant by the term "normative Unitarianism." That is why we have stood for all these years; that is what made us strong. We have grown when we have adhered to that legacy and those principles.

Let our hearts and minds and souls be taken captive by their vision. We have the holy task of spreading that message. Thus may we and our children, and our children's children, also know the way that leads to righteousness. So shall we become a holy people unto the Lord our God.

Unitarianism Begins, I
Michael Servetus

Unitarian history is difficult to trace because we don't begin with any one person. It can be traced back to Judaism and early Christianity. Modern Unitarianism, though, goes back to the early Reformation. It is an exciting story and it will unfold in two sermons. First, though, some background.

I.

The Reformation began on October 31, 1517 when Martin Luther nailed his 95 theses to the castle door at Wittenburg. Luther opposed many practices of the Roman Church, which he listed in those 95 statements. The Reformation was an advance in religious liberty, but it was not ready for Unitarianism. Unitarianism, in the historical context, has meant five things:

> **first**, one God in one person;
> **second**, belief in the goodness of human nature;
> **third**, the use of reason and conscience in matters of belief;
> **fourth**, salvation for all people;
> **fifth**, the obligation of moral responsibility.

Unitarianism has gone under many names but essentially it was a protest against two particularly hateful doctrines of Calvinism: total human depravity and predestination.

Calvin believed that we are totally depraved, capable of no virtue, no goodness, and no salvation except by the grace of God. We are all miserable sinners. Luther agreed with Calvin. Luther said,

> A man who has no part in the grace of God cannot keep the commandments of God, or prepare himself either wholly or partly to receive grace; he rests of necessity under sin.

The answer to that is that such a person, one who has no part in the grace of God, never existed. Seth Beach, a nineteenth-century historian, said,

> The doctrine of total depravity is perhaps the most revolting article ever formulated in the name of faith.... It denied the name of goodness to the kindly instincts, generous impulses, and high-minded endeavors which even in the savage it could not wholly ignore.... These things come from a corrupt heart. In the sight of God they had not the smallest moral worth.

Predestination was the doctrine that whether a person was destined for hell or heaven was decided at the moment of creation. Nothing that a person could do would alter that decision. It allowed no human freedom. Even in the words of Calvin it was "a horrible decree." It gave people no moral or spiritual possibilities. It denied human power to shape our conditions and destiny. It repudiated moral responsibility and everything the prophets pleaded for. It denied God's grace to the bulk of the species. Calvin said, "God, in saving some and condemning others, has no regard to their merits." Erasmus argued,

> It is written, "Choose you this day whom you will serve." It would be ridiculous to say to anyone, "Choose," when it was not in his power.

Unitarianism Begins, I

We must realize that Calvin and Luther were not reformers. They were reactionaries. Many improvements were being made in that time in theological circles. There was a growing tolerance and broadening of the definitions and interpretations of faith within the Catholic Church. Luther and Calvin reverted a thousand years back to the thinking of the fifth-century.

II.

Our story concerns two men. The first is John Calvin. He was born in Picardy on July 10, 1509. His father, Gerard Calvin, was an office-holder of some importance in the community and held some ecclesiastical offices. Gerard Calvin was esteemed as a man of considerable wisdom and prudence, and his wife was a godly lady.

John Calvin first was destined for the priesthood. At eleven he received a tonsure and was appointed chaplain of a cathedral. That required no duties, since he paid part of his handsome salary to a substitute to carry out his duties.

Calvin studied hard. He was especially good in grammar and philosophy. He advanced in the hierarchy. He was not yet ordained and his mind began to change. He questioned certain Roman practices and doctrines. He turned to law and studied at the University of Orleans.

Luther had published his 95 theses, and all Europe was rethinking its religious situation. There was no Reformation in France, but multitudes sympathized with it there. They wanted to improve the church by education, purer morals, better preaching, and a return to the primitive and uncorrupted faith.

Calvin was in sympathy with that trend. He began work on his *Institutes of the Christian Religion* and became a powerful influence in France. He puzzled whether to try to reform the Roman Church or to break from it. He decided to break away. His decision became known. He was arrested and served two short terms in prison.

Calvin came into contact with a number of different heresies during that period, all of which nauseated him. First were the

Anabaptists. They did not believe in infant baptism and preached that the soul slept after death. Calvin disagreed with those doctrines. Servetus, the Spanish physician, tried to persuade Calvin that the Trinity was unscriptural; but more of Servetus in a moment.

By 1534 Calvin was head of the Reformed movement in France. His life was in danger from the Inquisition, and he had to flee. He went to Basle in Switzerland, a center of learning, the Athens of Europe. There he published his *Christianismi Institutio* (*Institutes of the Christian Religion*), probably the greatest work in Protestant theology.

Calvin visited Geneva and was persuaded to remain. Farel, his friend, drew up 21 articles, and the populace was required to swear to them as their confession of faith. So began the theocracy Calvin was to establish.

Schools for the young were established, with Calvin's principles taught. Parents were forced to send their children. Anabaptists were driven from the city. All who dissented were expelled.

The Catholic Church was abolished completely by brute force. Farel took a bodyguard of storm troops and burst into a Roman church while the priest was at the altar celebrating the mass. He forced his way into the pulpit and fulminated against the Antichrist—that is, the Pope. Farel organized street gangs to raid the cathedral at service time and to disturb their devotions with screams, a quacking noise like that of ducks, and outbursts of laughter. The monasteries were violated, images of saints torn down and burned. History repeatedly has shown that a minority, even a small minority, can intimidate the majority by showing courage—providing that the majority lacks courage. In the end, the bishop handed over his see to the victorious Calvin and ran away without striking a blow.

Calvin was a man of tremendous strength of character. He wrote his *Institutes* at the age of 25, and never did he change or repudiate a single statement of it. Never once did he retrace a step or make a move in the direction of compromise. People who associated with him were either completely subordinate to him or they were against him. Not during the next 30 years did Farel, many years his senior, venture to contradict a word uttered by his junior.

III.

That was the city of Geneva in 1553. It was a city that loved freedom but then had no trace of it. It was ruled by a brutal and ruthless man who would tolerate no differences on any point, however trivial. There was no more liberty in Geneva. One will ruled everyone, and that will was John Calvin's.

At that time, in the year 1553, Miguel Serveto passed through the city. He was on his way to Italy, but he was compelled to stop overnight because of transportation difficulties. That involved a weekend and church attendance on Sunday was compulsory. Serveto went to church and was recognized. He was arrested immediately and held for trial.

Who was Miguel Serveto, known also as Michael Servetus? Servetus was a Spanish physician, born in the same year as Calvin, 1509. Like Calvin, he trained for the priesthood; like Calvin, he turned away from the Roman Church. He was an erratic genius, credited with a number of significant discoveries. He was a physician, theologian, scholar, and astrologer—astrology being a reputable science then. We know also that he discovered arterial circulation of the blood some hundred years before Harvey, and medical science now credits Servetus with that discovery.

Servetus had written a book in 1531 titled *De Erroribus Trinitatibus* (*Concerning the Errors of the Trinity*). He maintained that the Trinity was completely unscriptural and thus should be expunged from Christian belief. The book infuriated Calvin beyond description. The fact is that Servetus was right. The Trinity, however ancient and venerable a belief, simply is not in the Bible. There is nothing in the Bible to indicate that Jesus and the Holy Spirit were both gods, much less that all three were one. His book was banned. Servetus published another book, *Dialogues Concerning the Trinity*, the next year, and it, too, was banned.

Servetus then disappeared and changed his name to Michel de Villenueve. He studied medicine at the University of Paris and became a professor of anatomy. He was appointed physician to the Archbishop of Lyons and held that post for 12 years. He continued his theological studies and wrote *Christianismi Restitutio* (*Christianity Restored*). He sent a copy to Calvin, who recognized it as the work of the same hand that had written *De Erroribus Trinitatibus*. Calvin betrayed Servetus to the French Inquisition. Just before the trial Servetus escaped to go to Italy, a more enlightened country. He had to travel through Geneva, and on that trip he was apprehended.

Servetus then was in Calvin's power. Servetus had tried to convert the leader of the Reformed movement, and Calvin had sworn to have him killed, should he ever come within his grasp.

Servetus was imprisoned and brought to trial. The prosecutor was not a man equal to Servetus, and the trial was going in favor of Servetus. Then Calvin himself stepped in. Calvin avoided the limelight when it showed him in a bad light, and had had someone else arrest the Spaniard. But now the brilliant Servetus was winning. That was the more remarkable when we learn how the trial was conducted.

It was no trial at all in our sense of the word. It was only a chance for Servetus to recant, which he would not do. The trial continued through the months. Servetus was left to rot in prison, given neither clothing nor decent food. The once proud man grew into nothing more than a skeleton. They would provide him with no books, no pen or paper, no visitors with whom he might consult. No defense was allowed. Servetus argued against conducting a trial before the criminal courts when he was accused of nothing more than difference in theological speculation, but to that no attention was paid.

Servetus was not allowed to present his case, other than to answer yes or no to accusations and questions. Calvin stormed,

> Anyone therefore that really and seriously reflects upon the matter will acknowledge that it was his purpose to extinguish the light of sound doctrine, and overthrow all religion.

A more complete distortion of Servetus' purpose than that it would not be possible to make.

Finally, when Calvin took over the prosecution, he demanded that the trial stop and that sentence be rendered. Servetus had believed all along that right would triumph and he would be acquitted. Servetus had become more pitiable. His earlier petition for the plainest comfort and decencies of life had brought no response. He was more wretched than ever, shivering with cold and tortured by physical infirmities. His body was wracked with pain, eaten with vermin and lice. In a petition he besought the Syndics for the love of God to grant him some relief.

But the Syndics, the judges, decreed otherwise. He was found guilty. He was notified of the sentence only two hours before it was to be carried out. He was taken to the place called Champel, there fastened to a stake and burned alive, together with his written and printed books. Calvin related that when Servetus heard the sentence, Servetus stood like one stunned, drew deep sighs, wailed like a madman, and at length recovering himself kept beating his breast and moaning, *Misericordia, misericordia*—God have mercy on me.

IV.

Servetus had assumed that right would triumph. But the daily turn of existence does not heed such high principles when brought before the demoniacal ruthlessness of a man like Calvin. Justice and righteousness were submerged before the powerful will of John Calvin.

During Servetus' last hours he was beseeched by Farel to recant, but he would not. Calvin said he had not persecuted him for any wrong, but had for many years had warned him as kindly as he could. That may be the only time the word "kindly" was applied to Calvin. Calvin would not attend the execution. He said he had too tender a temperament and could not bear the cruelty.

Crowds accompanied Farel and Servetus to the execution. Along the way they kept urging Servetus to confess his fault. He replied that he was guilty of no fault, and prayed for God's mercy on his accusers. At the place of execution he fell on his face and continued in long prayer. Farel seized the opportunity to make an edifying address to the spectators. Again exhorted to say something, Servetus cried out, "O God, O God; what else can I speak of but God?" He was seated on a log with his feet touching the ground, his body chained to a stake, and his neck bound to it by a coarse rope. His head was covered with leaves and sprinkled with sulfur. His book was tied to his thigh. When the torch met his sight he uttered a terrible shriek, while the horrified people threw on more wood. He cried out, "O Jesus, son of the eternal God, have mercy on me!" Farel said to him that if he would change *one word* in the sentence and say, "O *eternal Jesus*, Son of God, have mercy on me!" he would withdraw the torch. But Servetus would not change a single word. After half an hour life was extinct. He had died and had not recanted.

And so justice and righteousness and mercy were trampled beneath the feet of Calvin. The noble Servetus, who wanted nothing more than to believe as his conscience dictated, now became one of the immortals. What the hemlock was to Socrates and the cross to Jesus, the fire was to Servetus.

The loving and gracious teachings of Jesus had been thrown aside in the name of Jesus. It would be well if it could be said that Calvin shortly received the punishment due him and that right quickly triumphed. But such was not the case. Calvin's brutality was not at an end. There was much more to come. Yet as Thomas Carlyle said, "The first of all truths is this, that a lie cannot endure forever."

We have seen something of the political and religious climate out of which Unitarianism arose as an organized movement. Unitarianism began at that time because, unfortunately for Calvin, he had not been able to foresee the effect of his outrageous travesty on every standard of right. Calvin was undone by an obscure professor of Greek literature in the nearby town of Basle.

That is the subject of the next sermon, when the story will be finished and you will learn of the encounter of John Calvin with the scholarly and shy professor of Greek literature.

Unitarianism Begins, I

Verdict by the Syndics of Geneva

(Excerpt from the sentence pronounced on Michael Servetus by the Syndics [Council of Judges] of Geneva, October 26, 1553)

Wherefore we Syndics, judges of criminal cases in this city, having witnessed the trial conducted before us at the instance of our Lieutenant [i.e., Calvin] against you "Michel Servet de Villeneufve" of the Kingdom of Aragon in Spain, and having seen your voluntary and repeated confessions and your books, judge that you, Servetus, have for a long time promulgated false and thoroughly heretical doctrine, despising all remonstrances and corrections and that you have with malicious and perverse obstinacy sown and divulged even in printed books opinions against God the Father, the Son and the Holy Spirit, in a word against the fundamentals of the Christian religion, and that you have tried to make a schism and trouble the Church of God by which many souls may have been ruined and lost, a thing horrible, shocking, scandalous and infectious. And you have had neither shame nor horror of setting yourself against the divine Majesty and the Holy Trinity, and so you have obstinately tried to infect the world with your stinking heretical poison....

For these and other reasons, desiring to purge the Church of God of such infection and cut off the rotten member, having taken counsel with our citizens and having invoked the name of God to give just judgment: having God and the Holy Scriptures before our eyes, speaking in the name of the Father, Son and Holy Spirit, we now in writing give final sentence and condemn you, Michael Servetus, to be bound and taken to Champel and there attached to a stake and burned with your book to ashes. And so you shall finish your days and give an example to others who would commit the like.

Unitarianism Begins, II

Sebastian Castellio

After John Calvin had Michael Servetus burned at the stake, he considered the matter ended. Servetus had denied the Trinity, a crime that Calvin could not see unpunished. After the execution, Calvin was reimbursed for his own expenses from the property of Servetus, and the rest of Servetus' money was turned over to the public treasury of Geneva.

Calvin was glad to see the matter finished. Melanchthon, Luther's colleague, wrote that it was a deed well done. In general the matter seemed to be ended. But Calvin had not reckoned on Sebastian Castellio, a mild-mannered professor of Greek literature in nearby Basle.

I.

Calvin defended the death of Servetus in a book. He called Servetus monstrous and attempted to show the dreadful harm his teachings would spread. But the damage was done. The death of Servetus, who had done nothing but disagree with Calvin's opinions, opened discussions that Calvin could not stop. Calvin expressed not the least regret at what he had done but showed loathing and contempt for Servetus as a very monster of iniquity, applying to him the foulest epithets. Seldom if ever in religious history has posthumous insult been more violent or odious, or more self-righteously used in the pretended service of God. Calvin called Servetus, among other things, *detestable infidel, rabid magician, great pest, vomit, obscene dog, stupid, ferocious beast*, and several other terms best not translated from the Latin.

Sebastian Castellio was a professor of Greek literature and a biblical scholar. He was born in 1515, near Geneva. At first he was friendly to Calvin, and Calvin made him rector of the Geneva school system. When it was found he did not believe certain parts of the creed and questioned the literal accuracy of the Bible, it became prudent for him to leave Geneva.

Castellio's reaction to the death of Servetus, whom he never knew personally, was immediate. He wrote Calvin, "If those thus butchered had been, I will not say horses, but only swine, every prince would have considered he had sustained a grave loss." "I doubt," he groaned, "whether in any epoch of the world's history so much blood can have been shed as in our own. . . . To seek truth and to utter what one believes to be true can never be a crime. No one must be forced to accept a conviction. Conviction is free."

Voltaire said the execution of Servetus was the first religious murder committed by the Reformation, and the first plain repudiation of the primary idea of that great movement.

Apologists for Calvin said that Calvin was a product of his age and Servetus merely a victim. That is not so. Castellio, Montaigne, and Erasmus were also of that day. It was not the blindness and folly of the time that sent Servetus to the stake, but the despotism of Calvin. Calvin must take his own blame.

Murmurs began to creep through Geneva. Calvin imprisoned people at every point and took up his pen to explain himself. He wrote his *Defense of the True Faith and of the Trinity against the Dreadful Errors of Servetus* when, as Castellio said, "his hands were still dripping with the blood of Servetus."

Calvin tried to justify himself. He wrote of the evils of the Catholic Inquisition. He said they sentenced true believers without giving them a chance to defend themselves and then had them executed in the most barbarous way. "What about you?" demanded Castellio. "Whom did you appoint to defend Servetus?" Of course Servetus was not allowed any defense at all.

Castellio pleaded with the town council for mercy. And Zerchintes, a friend of Castellio, wrote to Calvin,

> I avow that I, too, am one of those who would fain limit as far as possible the right to inflict capital punishment on account of differences in matters of faith, even where the error is voluntary. What determines my judgment in these matters is not only those passages of Holy Writ which can be quoted against the use of force, but also the way in which, here in Bern, the Anabaptists have been mishandled. I myself saw a woman of eighty dragged to the scaffold, together with her daughter, a mother of six children, these two women having committed no other offense than to repudiate infant baptism.... I deem it therefore advisable that the authorities should be rather unduly clement and considerate than to be over-ready to appeal to the sword.

II.

Castellio published his book *Concerning Heretics*. He showed opinions of the church fathers requesting leniency in the treatment of heretics. He even quoted Calvin himself, which threw Calvin into a rage. For Calvin had written, while himself under sentence for heresy in France,

> It is unchristian to use arms against those who have been expelled from the church, and to deny them rights common to all mankind.

Castellio wrote,

> It is absurd to use earthly weapons in spiritual warfare. The

> enemies of Christians are vices, and are to be overcome by virtues.... The cultivation of Christian character is neglected while Christians spend their time disputing speculative questions such as the nature of Christ, the Trinity, predestination, free will, the Eucharist and baptism. These are not necessary to salvation, and do not make a man better.

Calvin responded that liberty of conscience is "a diabolical doctrine." To make religion consist, as Castellio did, of a pure heart, the correction and reformation of life, is blasphemy, impiety, and sacrilege, since it undermines doctrine. Society must therefore expunge the impiety, even by death of those who profess it. Castellio responded,

> What do we really mean by the term "heretic"? Whom are we entitled to call a heretic, without being unjust? I do not believe that all those termed heretics are really such. When I reflect on what a heretic really is, I can find no other criterion than that we are all heretics in the eyes of those who do not share our views.
>
> We can live together peacefully only when we control our intolerance. Even though there will always be differences of opinion from time to time, we can at any rate come to general understandings, can love one another, and can enter the bonds of peace.

There was the crux of the whole matter: that people can love one another and still hold their individual beliefs. It seems to us incredibly simple. Yet in that day thousands were slaughtered in the name of religion. It took tremendous daring for Castellio to pen that message.

The butcheries, the barbarous persecutions—the blame for those did not fall on the heretics, but on their persecutors. In his *Manifesto on Behalf of Toleration* Castellio wrote,

> Men are so strongly convinced of the soundness of their opinions that they despise the opinions of others. Cruelties

and persecutions are the outcome of arrogance, so that a man will not tolerate others' differing in any way from his own views, although there are today almost as many views as there are persons. Yet there is not one sect that does not condemn all the others and wish to reign supreme. That accounts for banishments, exiles, incarcerations, burnings, hangings, the blind fury of the tormentors who are continually at work, in the endeavor to suppress certain outlooks that displease our lords and masters.

Castellio was a mild man and claimed to be a man sent up from the masses, not a prophet from God. But precisely because he had a humane heart, he could not restrain himself or confine his writings to academic inquiries. "However horrible these things may be," Castellio wrote Calvin,

> the sinners sin yet more horribly when they endeavor to wrap up their misdeeds in the raiment of Christ, and declare that they act in accordance with his will.
> Who would today wish to become a Christian when those who confess themselves Christians are slain by other Christians without mercy and are treated more cruelly than murderers and robbers? Who would wish to go on serving Christ when he sees how today anyone that differs in some paltry detail from persons who have wrested power to themselves is burned alive in the name of Christ, even though, like Servetus, he calls on Christ amid the flames and loudly declares himself a believer in Christ? What more could Satan do than burn those who call on the name of Jesus?

Calvin regarded all that as monstrously unjust. "A new heresy has been discovered," he stormed. "We must stamp out this burst of hell-fire before it spreads over the surface of the earth." Calvin demanded action. The new heretics must be killed and their books burned. Calvin wrote, "Freedom of conscience is a doctrine of the devil." "Better to have a tyrant, however cruel, than permit everyone to do what he pleases."

The warfare continued. Castellio demanded to know who had set Calvin up as an arbiter of public beliefs. "You began," he wrote, "by arresting your opponent, by locking Servetus in prison, and you excluded from the trial all except those who were the Spaniard's enemies." Servetus' only charge had been a difference in theological position. Servetus was not accused of any crime at all. Why, then, did Calvin appeal to the criminal courts? Differences in thought should be settled by the instruments of thought alone. Servetus had used nothing but rational arguments against Calvin. Calvin should have defended himself in the same way.

Calvin replied that it was his mission to save Christianity, and that a gangrenous limb must be amputated. To which Castellio replied, "There is nowhere in the gospels, nor yet in any moral treatise ever given to the world, the demand for such intolerance. Will you dare, in the last resort, to say that Jesus himself taught you to burn your fellow men?"

Then came Castellio's imperishable words: "*Who burns a man does not defend a doctrine, but only burns a man.*"

On raged the arguments. Castellio continued to inquire what crime Servetus had committed. He was not subject to Geneva law, had done nothing in that city except try to pass through it. There was not a legal shred on which to bring him to trial.

III.

Now, it must seem from those writings that surely Calvin would have been defeated instantly. All of Protestantism should have been converted by those writings. What was the effect? Nothing. Nothing at all. All of Castellio's writings had no effect. Why? Because his books were not allowed to go to press. Calvin throttled it by censorship and the conscience of Europe could not be reached. Calvin received cooperation because every tyrant in Europe realized the threat to his power.

Might prevailed over right. Calvin had the town of Geneva issue a demand to Basle that the professor be made to account for himself. Basle was frightened of Geneva and felt it better to sacrifice an individual than to run their heads against a wall.

Servetus had been silenced by fire. Now Castellio was silenced by censorship. Authority once again was maintained by terror. Against a reign of terror there is no appeal. Castellio had no alternative but to submit. His will was not broken, however, and he wrote, "Even if, for a season, truth is suppressed, no one can permanently coerce truth."

Calvin became more terrible than before. He gained more power, intensified by his crimes. Victory continued. Tension grew. Street brawls became frequent. Calvin then became a dictator. Confessions of treason were gained by the most atrocious cruelty, and all who resisted Calvin in the most trifling way were put to death.

But, strangely, the tide was turning. There were still men persuaded by Christianity, and they came to Castellio's defense. That incensed Calvin. He must now have revenge, whatever the pretext. He brought an accusation against Castellio. He accused him of being a libertine, a Pelagian, defender of all vicious, heretical, adulterous, thievish men, a Papist, blasphemer, skeptic, and Anabaptist, and charged that he had translated the *Dialogues* of Servetus into Italian from Latin. The last charge was true. Castellio was required to do translations as part of his job.

Calvin next accused Castellio of stealing firewood. He demanded that he be brought to trial. Castellio wrote to him,

> Woe unto those whom you lead if they are infected by your moods, and if it should prove that your disciples resemble their master. Some day truth will prevail and you, Calvin, will have to account to God for the abuse you have showered on me, to save whom, as to save yourself, Christ died. Is it possible that you are not ashamed, that you cannot remember Jesus' own words, "Whosoever is angry with his brother without a cause shall be in danger of the judgment"?

He went on to explore the foolishness of Calvin's charge that he had stolen the firewood. In fact he had taken driftwood from the

Rhine. That was a practice encouraged by Basle; the city paid a reward to those who retrieved the driftwood from the river, saving the bridges from possible harm. So that serious charge turned out to be utter nonsense.

But the charge was made against Castellio, foolish as it was. It was made by Bodenstein—remember that Calvin was too cowardly and never made those charges personally. The charges were palpably absurd but they were sufficient to bring him to trial.

The trial undoubtedly would have favored Castellio except for a circumstance that favored Calvin. It was discovered that a nobleman of Basle was in reality an arch-heretic who had assumed a noble disguise. That nobleman was a friend of Castellio's. The people of Basle turned against him when it was shown that he was also a friend of Bernardino Ochino. Ochino, later to become head of the Unitarian movement in Italy, was at that time a Franciscan monk, Vicar-General of the Capuchin order.

Castellio was dismissed from the University, and his health began to fail. Without money, his friends afraid to help him, he was starving to death and watching his family starve with him. He preferred even that to retraction of his efforts on behalf of toleration. He was forced to his bed at last, having been seized with uncontrollable vomiting. He had no will left, for he knew that Servetus' defender would receive Servetus' penalty: death by burning. And so, preparation for the trial was made. But on December 29, 1563, a merciful God granted Sebastian Castellio, aged 48, a peaceful death.

IV.

The citizens of Basle now realized they had lost a true patriot. They were horrified at the poverty-stricken condition of the nobleman. There was not a fragment of silverware in his house. Everything he owned had been sold to purchase food. His friends collected money to provide a funeral, pay his few debts, and care for his children. Now Sebastian Castellio had a posthumous moral triumph. The entire university faculty marched to the cathedral for the funeral, the coffin being borne on the shoulders of the students. Three hundred of his pupils collected money for a tombstone on which were chiseled the words, "To our renowned teacher, in gratitude for his extensive knowledge and in commemoration of the purity of his life."

Had conditions been more favorable for Calvin, Calvin's ideas might have engulfed civilization. Fortunately, they did not. For soon Europe rebelled against the tyranny over the mind that for so long had engulfed its people. Servetus became a *cause célébre*. Professor Matteo Gribaldi, a celebrated jurist from Padua, came to Geneva. He said no one should die for his opinions, however heretical; he gave reasons for his views and sought, in vain, a debate with Calvin on the subject. Laelius Socinus said Servetus was Abel crying to God, and that Cain—Calvin—would find no peace on earth. Bernardino Ochino declared that if Christ himself came to Geneva, Calvin would crucify him. One must go away from Geneva, he said, to find Christianity.

Descartes and Spinoza, influenced directly by Castellio, wrote books that freed people from the fetters of ecclesiasticism and tradition.

The name of Sebastian Castellio soon was forgotten. But his ideas did not perish in the tomb. Eventually his writings were published, though not until after John Locke had championed the same ideas. And so the name of Sebastian Castellio is all but lost to history. There are few who even know his name. He is honored by no memorials. No churches are named after him, not even rooms in churches. His writings are seldom read and almost impossible to obtain. There remains only that tomb in Basle, overgrown with weeds and neglected by a perfidious people.

But Castellio was on the side of truth. He is remembered by a few people. More important, his ideas are imperishable. His pleas for tolerance and respect, for simple kindness and mercy, have become cornerstones of Unitarianism. Castellio is, I think, the first person in history who could be called a Unitarian in the modern sense of the word.

Woodrow Wilson said, "I would rather be defeated in a cause that will one day triumph, than to win in a cause that must one day be defeated." Sebastian Castellio, then, must be pronounced the victor.

From Concerning Heretics, *by* Sebastian Castellio

When I consider the life and teaching of Christ who, though innocent Himself, yet always pardoned the guilty and told us to pardon until seventy times seven, I do not see how we can retain the name of Christian if we do not imitate His clemency and mercy. Even if we were innocent we ought to follow Him. How much more when we are covered with so many sins? When I examine my own life I see so many and such great sins that I do not think I could even obtain pardon from my Savior if I were thus ready to condemn others. Let each one examine himself, sound and search his conscience, and weigh his thoughts, words, and deeds. Then will he see himself as one who is not in a position to remove the mote from the eye of his brother before he has taken the beam from his own. In view of the many sins which are laid to us all, the best course, would be for each to look to himself, to exercise care for the correction of his life and not for the condemnation of others. This license of judgment which reigns everywhere today, and fills all with blood, constrains me... to do my best to staunch the blood, especially that blood which is so wrongfully shed,—I mean the blood of those who are called heretics, which name has become today so infamous, detestable, and horrible that there is no quicker way to dispose of an enemy than to accuse him of heresy. The mere word stimulates such horror that when it is pronounced men shut their ears to the victim's defense, and furiously persecute not merely the man himself, but also those who dare to open their mouths on his behalf; by which rage it has come to pass that many have been destroyed before their cause was really understood.

Now I say this not because I favor heretics. I hate heretics. But I speak because I see here . . . dangers. And the first is that he be held for a heretic, who is not a heretic. This happened in former times, for Christ and his disciples were put to death as heretics, and there is grave reason to fear a recurrence in our century, which is not better, but rather worse. The danger is greater because Christ said, "Think not that I am come to send peace on earth; I came not to send peace, but a sword. For I am come to set a man at variance against his father, and the daughter against her mother," etc. You see how easy it is for calumniators to say of a Christian, "This man is seditious. He sets a son at variance against his father and disturbs the public peace." Great care must be exercised to distinguish those who are really seditious from Christians. Outwardly they do the same thing and are judged guilty of the same crime by those who do not understand. Christ was crucified among thieves.

William Ellery Channing

A Study in Greatness

William Ellery Channing was one of the great religious thinkers of America. Let me tell you about him. He was born in Newport, Rhode Island, on April 7, 1780. He came from an old and prominent family, and from them he inherited his simple tastes, sweetness of temper, and warmth of affection. He also inherited a strong Puritan morality and strength of character. His father was a strict Calvinist, a disciple of Dr. Samuel Hopkins of the old school.

Young Channing was always interested in theology, but early on he could not abide Calvinism. Once he went to church with his father and heard Dr. Samuel Hopkins talk about the total depravity of human nature and how all of us are destined to spend eternity in Hell. On the way out of church, the father said to Dr. Hopkins, "Sound doctrine, Sir, sound doctrine." Young Channing trembled for his immortal soul, but he noticed that his father whistled happily on the way home. He saw that his father believed in total depravity, but he was kind and generous toward everyone, and always brought out the best in people. The contradiction bothered him.

The Price of Truth

I.

Channing became interested in theology and social problems, though in school he was not scholarly. At 12 he moved to New London, Connecticut to prepare for Harvard, where he came under the liberal influence of his uncle, Dr. Henry Channing, a noted preacher of that day.

Channing's interests at that time reflected a normal youth. He liked to climb the rigging of the Newport ships. He enjoyed good health, loved sports, flew kites, and once slept in a haunted house. He duly enrolled in Harvard College, along with the rest of the student body, 172 in number. He joined several clubs, but his thoughts turned to religion. He experimented with fasting, mostly in order to devote more time to study and less to eating, but the experiment undermined his health and he was never robust again.

Politics interested him. In his senior year at Harvard he organized the study body to pledge support to President Adams. In a petition, written mostly by our hero, the students declared that they bitterly resented the motives of the French, and approved without reservation the noble and disinterested policy of the United States. The petition read, "When we contemplate the French, our youthful blood boils within us. In defense of America we now solemnly offer the unwasted ardor and unimpaired energies of our youth to the service of our country."

At commencement time Channing's youthful blood apparently still boiled within him, and he was chosen class orator. There was a rule against political speeches, but that didn't bother him. Not only did he rail against the French but in closing he turned to face the faculty. He said to them, "But that I am forbid, I could a tale unfold which would harrow up your very souls." And with that declaration, to the applause of his listeners, he completed college.

He went to Virginia to recover his health and for the first time met respectable people who were Democrats. He learned to love their hospitality, their good manners, their warmth and color, and to hate their system of slavery.

Unfortunately the dire poverty of his family affected him so that he would not allow himself the luxury of decent clothes. He grew shabby in his appearance, and his natural shyness became almost pathological. He grew lonelier. He mortified the flesh, slept on the floor at night, ate scarcely enough to stay alive, and pored over his books night and day. Eventually he snapped out of that, but his health was permanently injured.

In 1800 the thin and pallid invalid returned to Newport. Two years later he went to Cambridge, but his questionable orthodoxy kept him from being called to the Brattle Street Church. He became pastor of the Federal Street Church in Boston, now the Arlington Street Church.

II.

His first sermon was preached on the text, "Silver and gold have I none, but such as I have give I thee." It was a good sermon, and contemporaries observed that a new light had appeared in the Boston firmament. He was ordained just after that. Participating in his ordination were the moderates—such stalwarts as Dr. Abiel Holmes, Dr. Tappan, and Henry Channing—not the orthodox. The moderates at that time didn't differ from the Calvinists in doctrine so much as in emphasis. Christianity to them was a religion of love and good conduct. To the old school, of course, that was heresy. Old Dr. Buckminster and Jedediah Morse complained bitterly but it did no good. Boston became the center of moderation, which came to mean more rational and less emotional, more moderate and less dogmatic. The phrase "Boston religion" brought shivers to the souls of good Calvinists.

In that atmosphere Channing continued to preach for more than ten years, insensitive to the theological storm brewing under his nose. His preaching still reflected the older beliefs. Just before the explosion took place he could say, "There is nothing in us to recommend us to God. Sinners as we are, we are vile in his sight. Our sins cry to God for unmingled vengeance."

But by 1815 the skies began to darken, the storm clouds gathered. The first shot was fired by Jedediah Morse. He complained that "Boston religion" was no better than Unitarianism, a movement of some note in England and suspected in this country. Morse wrote a pamphlet outlining the more odious doctrines of Unitarianism. Actually, there was little in common between English Unitarianism and the "Boston religion," but it was too late for facts to cloud the issue. The very Rev. Dr. Morse accused the Americans of being afraid to admit the true extent of their infidelity. He concluded his pamphlet with a call to all true Christians to separate the infidels and deny communion to them.

That was the heyday of pamphlet writing in this country, and Channing replied with one titled *A Letter to the Rev. Samuel C. Thatcher, on the Aspersions Contained in a Late Number of the Panoplist, on the Ministers of Boston and the Vicinity.* Briefly, Channing denied the odious charge of Unitarianism.

For three years the pamphlet war raged until in 1819 the full fury of the storm broke. One Jared Sparks, later President of Harvard, was being ordained in Baltimore and asked Channing to preach the sermon. That sermon, one of the two most famous sermons ever delivered in this country, was a powerful attack on the Trinitarian doctrine. It was titled *Unitarian Christianity* and became known as *The Baltimore Sermon*. It appealed to reason as the divine oracle in humanity. It appealed to the testimony of scripture, to the goodness of God, to the belief in the moral perfection of God. The loathing it caused among respectable Protestant ministers can hardly be imagined at this late date in history.

Conservatives flew to their writing desks. Pens scratched away at pamphlets into the small hours of the morning in a desperate attempt to refute this latest eruption of godlessness.

Biblical scholars came to Channing's rescue and the new liberalism spread like wildfire through Harvard. It horrified the older ministers of New England.

Channing's preaching became more powerful, his position clearer. Channing did take time then to marry Ruth Gibbs, a rich cousin, but he refused to use any of her money on the ground that clergymen were so commonly accused of marrying for money.

But on with the crusade. He turned to politics. A Thanksgiving sermon urged the overthrow of Napoleon. A sermon on war led to the organization of the Massachusetts Peace Society. He lectured at Harvard, and then journeyed to England, where he met Wordsworth and Coleridge, who influenced him greatly.

During all that time, Channing's reputation increased. Membership and church attendance grew, and a larger church had to be built. His salary was raised to $1,200 a year and he moved to fashionable Beacon Street. Honors were heaped upon him. He was made a member of the Harvard Corporation. Harvard gave him a D.D., and his church hired an assistant for him.

In 1823 a young man just then beginning his study for the ministry attended church and wrote his aunt Mary that "Dr. Channing is preaching sublime sermons every Sunday morning in Federal Street, one of which I heard last Sunday, and which infinitely surpassed Everett's eloquence." The young man was Ralph Waldo Emerson.

Channing became ever more liberal in social fields. In a sermon titled *Spiritual Freedom* he said, "I am shocked at the imprisonment of the honest debtor; and the legislation which allows a creditor to play the tyrant over an innocent man would disgrace, I think, a barbarous age. I cannot but remember how much of the guilt of the convict results from the general corruption of society." Such sentiments were not calculated to endear him to the men of position in the community.

One story from that period quotes a layman as saying, "When Dr. Channing used to preach about God and the soul, about holiness and sin, we liked him; that was Christianity. But now he is always insisting on some reform, talking about temperance or war. We wish he would preach the Gospel."

III.

Dr. Channing, to use a vulgar expression, had quit preaching and gone to meddling. But if they thought that was bad, there was worse to come.

To interrupt this narrative, his wife became sick, and she had to visit the West Indies for a cure. Channing accompanied her and there was reintroduced to the horrors of slavery. He began to write and preach like an obsessed person. He said the mental, moral, and spiritual degradation of slavery were beyond belief. He pleaded for conscience by the slaveholders but with no effect. He did not, though, identify with the abolitionists because of their belief in force.

When he returned to Boston, he found everyone was against him. His congregation considered him politically dangerous. His unreliable conscience had caused him to meddle with an institution whose fate affected New England's own textile industry. The wealthy people he served didn't care to have questioned the basis of their wealth.

The Abolitionists, on the other hand, considered him a tool of the moneyed interests. They spread the ugly rumor that he lived off the blood money of his brother-in-law, who owned a distillery.

Then one Samuel J. May, a Unitarian minister and a leader of the Abolitionist movement, persuaded Channing that the main reason the Abolitionist movement had gone astray was that such men as he refused to help. Channing listened and acceded to the argument.

And then, with Channing's support, the Abolitionist movement took on new life. Public opinion had found it easy to dismiss Garrison as a fanatic, Samuel May as a backwoods parson, Maria Chapman as a flighty woman. But the Rev. Dr. William Ellery Channing, minister of the distinguished Federal Street Church and acknowledged leader of the American Unitarian movement, was unassailable. The hysterical crowds had to pause and reflect.

Dr. Channing's congregation turned against him. They made cutting remarks to him in the street. They said the political bug had bitten him. Years later, Whittier wrote to Channing's son, "As to the matter of courage and self-sacrifice, very few of us have evinced so much of both as thy father. He threw upon the altar the proudest reputation in letters and theology, of his day."

Channing continued to plead against the use of force in the slavery issue but was drowned out. He continued unremitting appeals to reason and conscience, but slavery was neither a reasonable nor a conscionable business. He wrote, I must add, an open letter to Henry Clay urging that Texas not be allowed to come into the Union as a slave state. He is credited with having delayed for two years Texas' entrance into the union.

Channing never rested on the slavery issue. When Elijah Lovejoy was killed by a pro-slavery mob in Alton, Illinois, Channing persuaded the owner's of Boston's city government to open Faneuil Hall to convene a meeting to protest his murder. Channing spoke at the meeting and hecklers began their work. James T. Austin, the Attorney General of Massachusetts, rose to condemn the purpose of the meeting. He maintained that Lovejoy had died a fool and made the astonishing statement that the Alton mob acted in the same spirit as the fathers of the American Revolution.

That statement of Austin's inflamed the good men of Boston. Wendell Phillips rose to his feet and poured out such a flood of eloquence that the hecklers were shamed into silence and the meeting proceeded quietly to its close.

Channing still would not join the Abolitionists, who continued to label him a tool of the moneyed class. It was useless, he said, to combat slavery on a political basis. "The North has but one weapon," he insisted: "moral force."

IV.

The fight had taken a heavy toll on Channing's health, and he was unable to continue preaching. He took a leave of absence to rest in Vermont, but he got only as far as Bennington, where he was attacked by typhoid fever. He lingered there nearly a month and on October 2, 1842, at 62 years of age, he died.

His opponents would not rest. They passed the ugly rumor, demonstrably false, that he died in the bosom of the strict Calvinist faith.

An astonishing thing then happened. That frail little man became in death a veritable giant. The great men of two continents found it impossible to praise him enough. Sermons were preached in America and England. Whittier and Lowell wrote odes. His influence increased rapidly. His sermons and other works were collected and printed in huge volumes, which at once went through 22 large editions. Hundreds of thousands of those huge volumes are still found in libraries of Unitarian ministers and churches. His foreign reputation was hardly less than his domestic. George Bancroft introduced his writings into Germany, and Beethoven spoke of his debt to him.

In summing his character we are struck by its diversity. He spent his energies refuting the Trinity and restoring reason to its rightful place. He was the spiritual founder of the American Unitarian Association. He wrote pamphlets and preached sermons against all sorts of social evils. He was fearless and courageous to an extreme.

Physically Channing was short and slight. His eyes were unnaturally large, his voice wonderfully clear. His face was filled with devotional spirit. He was not a great pastor, and he lacked social tact. He never had the large numbers of friends we might expect. As a preacher, Channing was often criticized for failing to deal with the practical duties of everyday life.

Yet we consider him the guiding light of American Unitarianism and we revere him as one of our prophets. Why? Channing pleaded for reason in religion. He regarded Christianity as the one religion above all others, which could be brought to its full bloom only by use of reason. Just as the Wesley brothers brought Christianity to the people on an emotional basis, so did Channing present it so that it was intellectually acceptable.

Channing said the Bible must be taken as other books, and that our reason is the highest oracle given us by heaven. He single-handedly put orthodoxy on the defensive. He battled the orthodox over the doctrine of human nature, insisting that we are not born depraved and sinful but that each person has a divine spark within. That was the great battle between the Unitarians and the orthodox: not over the Trinity but over human nature. Channing persuaded huge numbers that human nature is intrinsically good.

He was the leading light behind the formation of the American Unitarian Association and always has been recognized as its spiritual founder.

Channing was a fine biblical scholar. His sermons are masterpieces of biblical erudition; not one of the orthodox could match him in biblical arguments. Channing's great mind matched the finest in philosophical and theological scholarship.

This was a man whose preaching moved multitudes. Read any biography of Emerson, Julia Ward Howe, Susan B. Anthony, or Samuel May, and you will see over and again the debt they announce to this giant.

Channing's enormous contemporary reputation was well deserved. He was far more than the comfortable purveyor of truisms, the sedative of the bourgeois conscience. Harriet Martineau said after meeting him, "You felt you were in a presence in which nothing that was impure, base, or selfish could breathe at ease."

Dr. Channing's peculiar gift seems to have been his ability to see more deeply than the mass of people, more deeply than the majority of intellectual leaders could do without losing their confidence. Freedom from religious dogma was mostly the result of his works. His was one of the finest and strongest voices raised against slavery. He fought the rum trade. He pleaded for the cause against children's sweatshops. He worked for better conditions for the poor; equality for women, including women's right to vote; better treatment of the blind; prison reform; reform of the insane asylums. He worked feverishly for everything that was for the common good. He was able to perceive that good because of his great learning and his great humanity.

Channing killed forever the old Calvinist doctrine that filled humanity with the spirit of the devil and degraded us into demonic monsters. He revived a religion that was destined to show humanity a gentler way.

There is a monument in the Public Gardens in Boston. It is a statue of William Ellery Channing. It faces the front door of the Arlington Street Church. That is the old Federal Street Church, which so many years prospered under his guidance. Written on the monument is the final tribute to his memory:

> *"He breathed into religion a new spirit,*
> *And proclaimed anew the divinity of man."*

FROM UNITARIAN CHRISTIANITY BY WILLIAM ELLERY CHANNING

We object strongly to the contemptuous manner in which human reason is often spoken of by our adversaries.... [T]he great question of [the] truth [of Christianity] is left by God to be decided at the bar of reason. It is worthy of remark, how nearly the bigot and the skeptic approach. Both would annihilate our confidence in our faculties, and both throw doubt and confusion over every truth. We honor revelation too highly... to believe that it calls us to renounce our highest powers....

In the first place, we believe in the doctrine of God's unity, or that there is one God, and one only. To this truth we give infinite importance, and we feel ourselves bound to take heed, lest any man spoil us of it by vain philosophy. The proposition, that there is one God, seems to us exceedingly plain....

We object to the doctrine of the Trinity, that... it subverts in effect, the unity of God.... "To us,... there is one God...." With Jesus, we worship the Father, as the only living and true God. We are astonished, that any man can read the New Testament, and avoid the conviction, that the Father alone is God....

We challenge our opponents to adduce one passage of the New Testament, where the word God means three persons, where... it does not mean the Father....

[The doctrine of the Trinity], were it true, must, from its difficulty, singularity, and importance, have been laid down with great clearness, guarded with great care, and stated with all possible precision. But where does this statement appear? From the many passages which treat of God, we ask for one, one only, in which we are told, that he is a threefold being, or that he is three persons, or that he is Father, Son, and Holy Ghost. On the contrary, in the New Testament, where, at least, we might expect many express assertions of this nature, God is declared to be one, without the least attempt to prevent the acceptation of the words in their common sense....

We believe in the *moral perfection of God*....We believe that God is infinitely good, kind, benevolent.... We believe, too, that God is just....

"God Is One!" Four Hundred Years of Unitarianism

This is the story of Francis David, known in Latin as Franciscus Davidis and in Hungarian as Davidus Ferenz. He was born in Kolozsvar, Transylvania, a principality bounded by the Carpathian Mountains in what is now northwestern Romania. Francis David was the son of a shoemaker. He studied to be a Roman Catholic priest and became literate in German, Hungarian, and Latin. He changed to Lutheranism and served a large Lutheran church in his hometown, Kolozsvar, or Cluj as it is in Romanian. He quickly became a leader of Lutheranism, was idolized by the people, and was appointed bishop. Dr. George Biandrata, court physician to King John Szigismund, then influenced him. Dr. Biandrata was liberal in his religion, and David became Calvinist and was appointed bishop in *that* church. David was the most eloquent debater, the most famous speaker in Transylvania, who knew his Bible from end to end.

Religious debates were popular then. They were formal disputations in which each side appointed its best debaters to present and defend carefully framed theses and antitheses, while stenographic reports were taken by the secretaries. The king himself often took part, and clergy and nobles attended in large numbers. Debates were as popular as jousts and tournaments were in an earlier time; or as popular as the most burning political questions are now. Debates about the nature of God, the real or symbolic presence of Christ in the communion, and the single or dual nature of Christ took place.

I.

Dr. George Biandrata and David held a conference in Torda to discuss religion. They adopted a Unitarian position and wrote a catechism. They wanted to restore the New Testament as the basis for all Christians to unite. In 1566 David published his book, *On the True and False Knowledge of the One God*, and from then his battle cry was *Egy az Isten!*—"God is One!" The book ridiculed the doctrine of the Trinity as absurd. That angered the orthodox but it appealed to the common people, the majority of whom were liberal. David dedicated the book to King John and wrote, "There is no greater piece of folly than to try to exercise power over conscience and soul, both of which are subject only to their creator."

Acrimony flew back and forth, and in January 1568 King John called the Diet of Torda, from which came his famous decree, *The Act of Religious Tolerance and Freedom of Conscience*. The king decreed,

> Preachers shall be allowed to preach the Gospel everywhere, each according to his own understanding of it. If the community wish to accept such preaching, well and good; if not, they shall not be compelled, but shall be allowed to keep the preachers they prefer. No one shall be made to suffer on account of his religion, since faith is the gift of God.

That was the first time in western history that a king was willing to allow his subjects a religion different from his. Now remember that was the same age in which the Inquisition was crushing out religious freedom, the same age when Calvin and his cohorts burned heretics at the stake, Luther wrote, "Let heads roll in the streets," and the massacre of St. Bartholomew's Day slew 30,000 Protestants in France.

King John called a general synod of ministers of both Hungary and Transylvania to meet in his palace. Five debaters led by David and Biandrata on the Unitarian side were against six on the Calvinist side, headed by Bishop Peter Melius. It was the greatest debate in Unitarian history. In the king's palace were gathered the whole court and great throngs of ministers and nobles. The formal debate began at 5 a.m. on March 8, 1568. It lasted ten days and was conducted entirely in Latin.

The Calvinists appealed to the authority of the Bible, the creeds, the church Fathers, and the orthodox theologians. David appealed to the Bible alone. The debate began with heat and got hotter. Bishop Melius said in his opening statement, "If I win this debate, you will be executed." David replied in his opening, "If I win this debate, you will be given the freedom due to every son of God." On the ninth day the Calvinists asked not to be forced to listen further, but King John refused them. The debate ended the next day with victory for the Unitarians; or, as the Calvinist historians said, "without any profit to the Church of Christ."

David covered himself with glory. He returned to Kolozsvar in complete triumph. Crowds received him and because there was not room enough in the cathedral for the crowds, they made him mount a large boulder at a street corner to speak to them. That boulder is preserved by the Unitarians of Kolozsvar as a sacred relic. It is inside the great Unitarian church in Kolozsvar. So great was his eloquence that the whole town became Unitarian. The remaining Lutherans left Kolozsvar in disgust. Kolozsvar was then a Unitarian city. All its churches and schools and all members of the City Council were Unitarian. Francis David, former Lutheran bishop, former Calvinist bishop, now became Unitarian bishop, the head of all our churches.

II.

The Calvinists wrote furiously against the Unitarians. Where they held power they persecuted and drove out Unitarians. King

John summoned them and said if the Calvinists didn't believe in freedom of conscience, they had better remove to some other country. He said, "We wish that in our dominions there be freedom of conscience, for we know that faith is the gift of God, and that one's conscience cannot be forced."

That was the golden age of Unitarianism. It spread rapidly among the nobility, clergy, and peasants. Generals, judges, and councilors became Unitarian. Professors and students converted. The orthodox abandoned even their monasteries, which the Unitarians turned into universities. The press spread the message. Tracts, books, and articles were published—in Latin for the scholars, in Hungarian for the common people. There were over 500 Unitarian churches in the Kingdom. Note that Unitarianism was *not* the official church. There was freedom for all churches alike. Dr. Earl Morse Wilbur wrote,

> It is worthy of note that at the only time in history when there has been a Unitarian king on the throne, and a Unitarian government in power, they used their power not to oppress other forms of religion, nor to secure exceptional privileges for their own, but to insist upon equal rights and privileges for all.[3]

And then, on March 15, 1571, at not quite 31 years of age, King John died. Unitarianism continued to spread, but the familiar pattern of persecution began. A Lutheran bishop persuaded the government, headed then by a Roman Catholic, to behead two prominent Unitarians as heretics. Wealthy Unitarians protested, and three Calvinists were condemned to death as murderers. The Calvinists panicked but the Unitarians interceded, saying they did not want revenge, and a fine was levied. That accomplished the goal, and the Calvinists were more peaceful after that.

The orthodox intrigued with the new king to convince him that Unitarians were heretics and therefore disloyal. The Unitarians were forbidden to publish anything and were expelled from court.

---

[3] *Our Unitarian Heritage*, p.231.

"Innovators" were banished, with imprisonment or death decreed for blasphemy.

Biandrata, still the court physician, managed to improve things a little, and in 1576 the office of Unitarian bishop was given legal recognition. The next king was less tolerant, and more restrictive measures were enacted. The Unitarian bishop was forbidden to visit his churches. The king invited the Jesuits into the kingdom in 1579, and the reign of terror began.

Francis David remained bold, and Biandrata warned him that his boldness would cause persecution. David refused to remain silent, saying it would be hypocrisy to do so. He kept speaking and was imprisoned in his own house. He escaped and went to the cathedral to preach a final sermon, warning the people of persecution to come and eloquently defending the Unitarian doctrine. It was his last sermon, and he closed it by saying, "*Whatever the world may say, it must some time become clear that God is but one.*" "Egy az Isten"—God is One! Then he was arrested.

David's confinement was made worse. Not even his family was allowed to visit him. He was not allowed treatment for his illness. Too weak to stand, he was taken to court in a wagon. While he argued still for Unitarianism, the Jesuits who counseled the king pronounced his teachings as damnable blasphemy. Friends asked for mercy, but the Jesuits wanted blood. David, sick and pitifully weak, could hardly move hand or foot, and he had to be lifted and carried from one place to another. Fearing to burn so famous a man, they condemned him to life imprisonment. He was locked in a cell in the old damp castle at Deva. His illness was not treated, and he died of neglect on November 15, 1579. His body was thrown into an unmarked grave, whose location is unknown to this day.

III.

David was an untiring student of the Bible. He had great personal courage and never shrank from taking the next step in his thinking—not pleasant to those who want a reformer to think something and never change his mind. He was not a man to think one thing in heart and keep silent about it in the pulpit. Neither bribes nor threats could move him from faithfulness to the truth as he saw it. He still is revered throughout Hungary and Transylvania as a man of God.

After David's death, there was no effective leadership among the Unitarians, and Calvinist persecution joined the Jesuits. Unitarians were put to death on false charges of treason. Their churches and the homes of the wealthy were burned, pillaged, and defaced.

In 1595 Prince Szigismund surrendered his government to the Emperor Rudolph, and the bloody General Basta was sent to exterminate all Unitarians from Transylvania. Unitarian churches were taken away and given to the orthodox. The chief Unitarian Church in Kolozsvar, David's own church, was given to the Jesuits. General Barbiano, a Roman monk turned soldier, declared he would kill every grown person in Hungary and Transylvania who refused to convert to Roman Catholicism. So cruel was General Basta that for generations his name was used to frighten children. Basta hung ministers up to smother in the smoke from piles of their own burned books. He flayed others alive. Soldiers pillaged houses of Unitarian nobles, ravished their wives and daughters. The Unitarians put up a brave and noble battle, but they were no match for the superior armed might of the cruel Jesuits. General Basta became more cruel than ever, but Unitarians continued to worship in private homes. Wasted as they were by war and persecution, they stuck wonderfully fast to their faith under the leadership of fearless and faithful bishops.

Oppressive laws were enacted. Much of the persecution was not literally against Unitarianism as such. When religious bigotry wishes to pursue its course of persecution, it usually finds another pretext. Treason is a convenient excuse to close printing houses and churches. The persecution continued another century and a half, and Unitarians watched as one after another heroic leader was beheaded, banished, despoiled of his goods, and treated in the most shameful ways. They saw their people stoned in the streets, their children mobbed, wives pilloried, and property confiscated.

But the Unitarians survived because of their heroic faithfulness. They developed intense loyalty to their religion. Unitarians in Transylvania flourished in the deeper spiritual meaning of that word. They risked persecution to help those already persecuted. They took them into their homes and fed them when their homes had been burned or sacked. They worshiped privately when it was a criminal offense to do so. Their dedication came from deep travail, from fighting for something more valuable than life itself, from placing honor above material well being, from a dedication to God that no earthly prince could subvert. The Calvinists and Jesuits took over their churches and schools and confiscated their goods. They reduced the nobility to peasantry but the Unitarians held it better to be a peasant with honor than a nobleman without it.

IV.

And there it remains today: Unitarianism as a strong peasant movement, the nobility and aristocracy still Calvinist or Catholic. They know their history well and recount to each generation the stories I have just told. A parishioner in Youngstown, Ohio came to America from Transylvania. He spoke little English but he was a devoted member of the Unitarian church. Once I asked why he attended our church when there were Hungarian churches in town that spoke his language. His reply was simple: "I am *Unitarius*. This is my church." Then in his broken English he recounted with obvious pride the legends about Davidus Ferencz.

That is our heritage. That is how our religion came to us as a free movement, filled with the rich tradition and heroes and mighty struggles of ages now gone, but which, as we remember them and take them to our hearts, build foundations for our spiritual well-being.

In Transylvania, Unitarianism has, in the face of cruel and almost continuous oppression, maintained an unbroken and heroic existence for more than four centuries. There are about 85,000 Unitarians there today. They elect bishops to oversee their spiritual needs. They flourish, build new churches, and hold firm in their faith. The churches are crowded, and the young are devoted to the religion of their ancestors.

In the museum in Torda hangs an enormous mural. It covers the whole wall. It depicts the famous debate between David and Melius, the debate that took place between March 8 and March 18, 1568. Reproductions of that mural are common in the churches and homes of Transylvania.

And the Unitarian peasant, sitting at home high in the Carpathian Mountains, after a day's work planting and plowing, reads the Bible, teaches doctrine and scripture to the children. The parent recounts the heroic struggles of the people remembering the great saints of their religion: Francis David, George Biandrata, and King John Szigismund. The hope is voiced that someday there will arise another champion who will enable everyone to sit under their own vine and fig tree with none to make them afraid.

In every home is repeated often the words that are carved on every church, the words of Francis David: *Egy az Isten*—God is One.

Act of Religious Tolerance and Freedom of Conscience
issued by King John Szigismund, March 18, 1568

His Majesty, our Lord, in what manner he—together with his realm—legislated in the matter of religion at the previous Diets, in the same manner now, in this Diet, he reaffirms that in every place the preachers shall preach and explain the Gospel each according to his understanding of it, and if the congregation like it, well, if not, no one shall compel them, for their souls would not be satisfied, but they shall be permitted to keep a preacher whose teaching they approve. Therefore none of the superintendents or others shall abuse the preachers, no one shall be reviled for his religion by anyone, according to the previous statutes, and it is not permitted that anyone should threaten anyone else by imprisonment or by removal from his post for his teaching, for faith is the gift of God, this comes from hearing, which hearing is by the word of God.

We wish that in our dominions there be freedom of conscience; for we know that faith is the gift of God, and that one's conscience cannot be forced.

Emerson and Compensation

Let me introduce you to Ralph Waldo Emerson by way of one of his writings. He considered compensation his most important idea. It was published in 1841 in his first series of essays. Emerson was then 38 years old and had a solid reputation as a lecturer and philosopher. Compensation was a constant theme in his essays and lectures all his life.

Emerson was so agile a thinker that a list of his major themes would take a long time. Let me mention his three most important themes, though.

First, self-reliance. That was his earliest theme and, simply stated, he meant that we each contain God within us. Our destiny is fulfilled and our happiness attained by being true to that divinity within us. Emerson did not mean by self-reliance just "do your own thing." If you look within and find only yourself, he said, that is pride, which is the nearest thing to atheism.

His second major theme was transcendentalism. That is the German philosophy of Idealism. Emerson did not like the term "transcendentalism." Idealism is the philosophy that God is Absolute Idea, or Pure Intellect. Nature is God expressing himself. The world basically is thought or idea. We are the juncture of nature and idea. Our intellect is a small or miniature manifestation of God. We are the point at which nature is self-conscious and can reflect on itself. Emerson's transcendentalism came to full bloom in his first published work, *Nature*. That book, by the way, was published anonymously in 1836. It had a printing of 500 copies and took seven years to sell out.

I.

Emerson's third major theme was compensation, about which I want to talk in some detail.

Emerson early in life became devoted to the idea of compensation. Let me give you some background. "Compensation" reflects his background of Puritanism, which taught that every wrong is righted, every sin repaid, every indulgence punished. You see there something of a clockwork universe, a mechanical world in which every action has an opposite and equal reaction, every *quid* its *quo*. The proud are humbled, and toils and struggles all are rewarded.

Emerson was taught the hard lessons of life both by his stern Aunt Mary Moody Emerson and by his own experience. His aunt Mary was his primary mentor, since his father died while he was a child and his mother was not a strong person emotionally.

Emerson was reared in poverty. When his father died the family had to sell his library. His mother had to take in boarders; and later she secured lodgings for the family only by doing menial housework. So much for those who think Emerson was born with a silver spoon in his mouth.

As a child, Emerson was given to various ills. He had weak lungs and complained of "a mouse gnawing at my chest." Pneumonia was commonplace in his family and his first wife died of it. His eyes were defective, and he required optical surgery, the same operation that blinded other people. His legs were lame. Several of his brothers and sisters died of various illnesses, and one was mentally defective.

Emerson was painfully shy and almost pathologically modest. He was never romantically involved until he met Ellen Tucker, when he was 24 and she was 16. She became ill before they were married, and she died only 19 months after their marriage. She was an invalid the whole time.

Yet none of that caused Emerson to become bitter. He considered suffering as the fire that tempers the metal. He once said to Edward Everett Hale of a divinity student, "Yes, he has many fine qualities. Now if only something would go wrong—if he should become ill, or if his father would become bankrupt, or if some other tragedy would befall—then all will be well with him, but not otherwise." In his *Divinity School Address* he referred to "the nonchalance of boys sure of a dinner."

II.

I said Emerson was something of a Puritan. He was a stern man. He did not like loud laughter. He always dressed in black. He did not like frivolity and would not abide card playing. Jokes about death he considered in the worst taste. He was not given to small talk. When someone said of him that he was not a warm person, he replied that he had never intended to be a substitute for the kitchen stove.

In his thinking, though, he was far from Puritanical. He believed in the innate goodness of human nature. He considered the doctrine of original sin the worst folly. He saw goodness everywhere. Nature was a delight. The song of the thrush was an angelic choir, and the spring flowers finer than Rembrandt's art. The Concord woods were cathedral arches. He saw in the mass of people only potential heroes and always brought out the best in everyone. A washerwoman in Boston always attended his lectures at Faneuil Hall. A newsman noticed her one day and asked her if she understood Mr. Emerson. "Not a word," she replied, "but I love to see him standing up there thinking everyone else is just as good as he is."

George Minot, a farmer who lived in Concord, saw Mr. Emerson pause in thought in the road before his house one day.

Mr. Minot said to his nephew, "Charley, that man ain't like other men. He's like Enoch; he walks with God and talks to his angels."

One more story. After Mr. Emerson resigned the pastorate at Second Church in Boston he preached regularly for two years at the Follen Church in East Lexington. Once he had another minister preach there, whom he hoped the congregation would secure as their regular minister. Miss Elizabeth Peabody asked a parishioner why they didn't call the man to be their minister. The parishioner replied, "Oh, Miss Peabody, we are a very simple people here, and cannot understand anybody but Mr. Emerson."

III.

Now we consider the essay *On Compensation*. Emerson, of course, was trained as a clergyman. He was descended from a long line of New England clergy, going back to the founding of Concord in 1635 by Peter Bulkeley. When he left the parish ministry, he continued his regard for religion. Indeed, his essays all reduce themselves to sermons and can be understood only as such.

His essay *On Compensation*, for example, is his exploration of the way in which God's will works in human activity. He said that there are stern laws of God that make themselves known to us. There are physical laws, as we know; but Mr. Emerson believed there are also unchanging moral laws. They are more difficult to understand, but they are there, working silently and surely. Like physical laws, we can ignore them or violate them, but we do so at our peril. The Ten Commandments are an example of moral laws.

The fundamental law of God is the moral law, or what Emerson called compensation. The qualities society calls virtues are not arbitrary rules laid down by priests or handed by God to Moses on Mt. Sinai. They are the wisdom of the ages. The values we cherish have been discovered through a long and impressive history of human experience. We have been taught that some things are good and others are bad; some ways are right and others wrong. You can violate the moral law, but not with impunity. We may attempt to play fast and loose with nature, but, as he said, nature cannot be cheated. "The dice of God are always loaded," he wrote, by which he meant that morals are not random or chance. We get what we deserve, in exact proportion. We may yield to the vices—pride, lust, gluttony, sloth, avarice—but we always pay the price. "Take what you want," said God, "and pay for it."

Mr. Emerson often is criticized for seeing things too simply. We see that many people enjoy the fruits of ill-gotten gains. Those who scheme and plot to deprive others often are adored by society and given seats of honor. But is that really so? Is it not the case that in the end our troubles are caused by our own vices, that evil is of our devising, and that good comes to those who are kind, generous, patient, honest, and loving?

It is easy to make a case against that; but consider the question, what is most important in life? If you arrange a scale of values, surely you will put character at the top. And how does one achieve high character? Is it not by sacrifice, commitment, loving devotion to others, and service to the common good? Is character ever achieved by anything other than hard work, foregoing temporary pleasures for a distant and greater good, and by selfless concern for others?

Of course we suffer. Of course we endure agony, pain, and toil. No one ever promised that life would be easy. You think of those more favored by nature, who have all the advantages you yearn for; but if you will ask them you will see that, in the first place, they are not so well disposed as you imagine; and, in the second place, that what good they have, they earned in the marketplace of toil and care.

What are the truly good things in life? Character surely is at the top of the list. Right alongside are such qualities as wisdom, courage, justice, honor, and integrity. But how are those treasures acquired? Can you suppose that anyone ever attained them easily or without struggle?

There is a balance in nature. As Thomas Paine said of liberty, what we obtain easily we esteem lightly. Nature knows how to put a proper value on its goods, and what is ennobling and productive of true happiness is won only with the greatest difficulty.

We are undone because we do not attend to those truths. We are cajoled by modern society to treasure most of all things that are the least worth. We want fame, riches, and comforts. But suppose you had them: then what? Would a wall filled with diplomas, honorary degrees and titles bring any joy in the lonely hours? Fame and wealth are elusive; for if you had a million dollars you would want ten million; and if you had ten million there would always be someone with more, of whom you were envious. We are burned with desire for pleasure, but pleasure is not the same thing as happiness and may even be the opposite of it.

Life is applied theology. Doctrines are stiff and formal. We know God by looking about, by examining our own lives. We do have a theology, whether we know it or not. Perhaps we cannot articulate our theology, but there are values and principles, a belief system, that guide us; and that is what theology is.

Observing nature teaches us religion. From science we learn cause and effect, chemical and mechanical laws. Those laws operate in the moral sphere, too: one thing attracts, another repels. One thing complements the other. All things fit into a whole. All are important and nature plays no favorites. Emerson saw a link between physical and moral nature: they are all part of the same process. The same laws operate throughout. Everywhere there are checks and balances. Upright character, honesty, gratitude, kindness produce inevitable results, just as the combination of oxygen and hydrogen in certain proportions produces water. Every act has unending consequences. All acts are related because they are part of a whole.

Judgment is in this world, not the next. Emerson had no use for preachers who talk of judgment in the next world, who say that good is rewarded and evil punished later. No. It happens now. We think to be happy and find compensation in heaven, but justice is done in this world. The thief or embezzler, we think, enjoys the fruits of his sin, but that is not the case. In fact the thief steals from himself; the liar deceives himself most of all.

Let me give you a simple example of how the moral law works relentlessly. Every sin you commit weakens your character and disfigures the soul. Sin enough, and finally character is destroyed. If that is the case, remember that you did it to yourself. No one else can do that to you.

I was the victim of a hit-and-run accident. Someone dented my right rear fender and did not make amends for it. He gave me a false identity and address. It cost me $150 to have the damage repaired. For that $150 I suffered annoyance and a financial loss; but for that $150 someone else compromised his integrity. He made of himself a liar, a cheat, a thief. So he suffered the greater loss. There is no lasting enjoyment from the promotion we gain by cheating; no satisfaction from victories won by deceiving other people.

So in our lives compensation works its inevitable course. Every excess causes a defect. Every sweet has its sour, every evil its good. If we overeat, we get a stomachache; so indigestion is the stomach's way of enforcing morality.

By extension we see that immorality produces bitter rewards. Those who gain by violence can keep their gains only by violence. Those who spend their lives in love are loved in return. What greater reward is there than to earn the love of friends?

IV.

Emerson reminds us of what we already know. God is everywhere. "God reappears with all his parts in every moss and cobweb." "What is there of the divine in a load of bricks?" he asked: "all; everything." God is not limited to an appearance now and then in history, or in consequence of fervent prayers. God is always present, in every soul, in every deed. Every human relation has a silent partner, and our lives are improved significantly as we remember that.

Emerson was not oblivious to evil. He saw it all about him, and he was not immune to its temptation. "There is a crack in everything God has made," he said. Perfection is not the common lot. Yet evil is a blemish to be removed, a task to be fulfilled, a duty that summons our creative powers.

The Price of Truth

The primary harm of doing something wrong simply is the knowledge that we have done it. "Commit a crime," he said, "and the earth is made of glass." Commit a crime and the earth is made of glass: we are hounded by conscience, the voice of heaven within us. There are people who repudiate conscience, but that is a terrible fate. Little by little we are able to set aside the judgment of our higher selves and the soul is encrusted with layer after layer of evil. "We all have sinned and fall short of the glory of God," as the Good Book says;[4] but "every man in his lifetimes needs to thank his faults." It is by error that we become better.

So Emerson demonstrated the truth of the moral law, of compensation. We see compensation most clearly in Emerson himself. He struggled and toiled. He knew want and privation. Integrity, honor, courage, and wisdom earned him the love of all who knew him. He had no enemies. He is cherished as the greatest American thinker, and rightly so. If we will follow those same ways of honor, integrity, wisdom, and courage, if we will take our hardships as blessings, and see that we leave a goodly heritage: then we, too, will see the just rewards of our lives, and we will feel the grace of God descend on us.

Emerson wrote once,

> An institution is the lengthened shadow of one man; as, the Reformation of Luther; Quakerism, of Fox; Methodism, of Wesley; Abolition, of Clarkson.

If we Unitarians, who owe so much to Emerson, would aspire after greatness, we could hope no more than that our institution would be the lengthened shadow of Ralph Waldo Emerson.

---

[4] Romans 3:23.

Why Pray?

It would be an unusual form of worship that did not include prayer. We take prayer for granted. But why do we pray? What do we expect it to do for us?

I.

Prayer binds us, even though we sit alone with our thoughts. Thus, when we say the Lord's Prayer, we are conscious of repeating a prayer spoken through so many centuries and by people the world over. Everyone with any Christian associations is familiar with it. Thus that prayer, said to have been spoken by Jesus, binds us not only with his spirit but also with all in the past who have repeated it, and with people of so many different denominations in so many countries. It reminds us of our ties with the larger Christian community.

We don't know whether Jesus ever spoke that prayer but certainly it expresses much of his sentiment. In fact, it is a Jewish apocalyptic prayer, a plea, perhaps, for this world to end and a new order to be established.

The same advantage attaches to the prayer of St. Francis: "Lord, make me an instrument of thy peace." It is a beautiful prayer, asking that we may bring love to replace hate, union instead of discord, truth to replace error, hope to replace despair.

Another prayer familiar and well loved by so many is that of James Montgomery, the Scottish hymn writer:

> *Prayer is the soul's sincere desire,*
> *Uttered or unexpressed,*
> *The motion of a hidden fire*
> *That trembles in the breast...*
>
> *Prayer is the simplest form of speech*
> *That infant lips can try,*
> *Prayer, the sublimest strains that reach*
> *The Majesty on high.*

Prayer reminds us of the need to pull aside and reflect on what we are doing with our lives. We are too much with the world. We go about being busy but with little thought of what we are trying to do. Most people want just to get along from one day to the next, do their job well, save money for the necessaries, plan a holiday now and then, and perhaps indulge in some hobbies or reading.

But toward what end? Is there not some higher calling to which we are responsive? There are impulses within us that cry out for expression. Prayer tries to bind us to those higher impulses and remind us of the nobility of the human spirit and perhaps our connection with God.

II.

Sometimes we discuss the question of God's existence. Is there a God? If so, what is God like? We ask, with Micah, what doth the Lord require of thee? How ought we to worship God? The Roman worship is hallowed with centuries of authority. The Anglican worship has its venerable *Book of Common Prayer*, one of the monumental accomplishments in the English language. Many other denominations cite authority from the Bible or great leaders. Religion seems to add so much confusion to the very questions we want to have simplified.

Why Pray?

Prayer puts all those questions and discussions aside. Prayer is an individual approach to God. It is the pulling apart from the busy-ness of the world, from the myriad distractions of life, to contemplate what is beyond us.

Prayer is our recognition that somehow, in some mysterious way, we are connected to forces beyond us. We do not understand them, but we do not have to understand them to draw strength from them. There is much that is hidden. We do not have road maps to guide us, nor almanacs that answer the deep questions. But we have access to a resource that can be ours. It is a resource that we can know, at least partly, and as we open ourselves to its influence, we sense something good is added to our lives.

Prayer to the religious person is based on the conviction that something in this universe is responsive to the humble heart, the contrite spirit. In a curious way, too, we recognize that there is an element of danger. We can call forth destructive powers. We are capable, every one of us, of evil. We read the stories of horror in the paper or see them on the television, and we shudder at the wickedness of human undertakings. Daily we are confronted with ugliness and malignity that stun the imagination. We see the most brutal kinds of destruction, some of it organized by governments or insurgent groups, some by individuals. Some of those individuals are only children, but they can be as deadly with a gun in their hands as any adult. It is a terrible fact of modern technology that immense destructive power can fall into hands of nearly anyone with strong motivation.

In that horror and tragedy portrayed daily, we are not reading fiction but a reality more ghastly than we have known. The stories are made more horrible yet by the knowledge, hidden in our unconscious, that we, too, are capable of that kind of evil. We have not killed, but we have wished for the death of people. We have schemed and plotted every kind of dread.

Prayer helps us overcome that unwanted side of our own nature. We recognize that against the destructive forces there are to be found within us urgings toward love, creativity, beauty, and compassion. Our hearts yearn for poetry and music and companionship.

III.

We are dedicated to the proposition that the religious life is desirable. It opens doors to a better world, a kingdom that Jesus said lies within. That better world is threatened by poverty, war, disease, and brutality that corrupt the spirit. But we need to recognize, too, that there are other, more subtle forces that can corrupt us. Our lives may become dissipated in formality and routine. The heart can turn cold. When love dies, faith is cold.

Our world wants to progress, and that usually involves increased production of goods or services. We have available to us reliable automobiles, high-quality television, stereo music, and inexpensive copies of all the great classic books. We have live performances of ballet, opera, symphony, lectures, and drama. There are fine universities and libraries.

We enjoy those things, and we are pleased that we can participate in such cultural advantages. But the spirit cries for something more. We want to become morally and ethically responsible people. We want to understand what meaning our lives have.

James Luther Adams, one of our great Unitarian thinkers, said,

> The distinguishing act of the religious person is worship, and the essence of worship is prayer. Other activities, to be sure, are of concern to the religious person. But prayer is the characteristic act of the religious life.

A problem with prayer for sensible people is that entirely too much is claimed for it. Prayer can be a great source of strength or a source of self-delusion. It can give us courage, or it can be a substitute for duty. We see sports participants praying for their side to win, which implies a curious notion of God. People pray for God to do for them what they ought to do for themselves. There is a Russian proverb: "Pray to God, but row to the shore."

Dean Inge once mocked that foolish belief in such use of prayer. He spoke with glee about receiving a letter from a lady who disagreed with one of his articles. "I am praying for your death," she wrote. "It may interest you to know that I have been successful in two other cases."

One of the oddest stories about prayer, I think, was the attempt of Sir Francis Galton, an English scientist of the nineteenth-century, to demonstrate the falsity of prayer. He wrote a paper titled *Statistical Inquiries into the efficacy of prayer.* It was published in 1872 and caused a furious debate. He gathered statistics to show that monarchs whose good health and longevity are constantly prayed for by loyal subjects, actually enjoyed on average a shorter life span than other rich men. His statistics showed that the nobility, who are also prayed for, are more prone to insanity.

Sir Francis said that if there were any material advantages to be gained by prayer, they would long have been observed by those sharp-eyed men who calculate insurance risks. Yet Galton pointed out that insurance companies did not reduce their rates for missionary ships, which were just as likely to sink as slave ships. He then noted, as a *coup de grace*, that if clergy really believed what they preached, they would not need to put lightning conductors on churches.

A curious side to that report was that Galton recognized that prayer has emotional values. He held family prayers and was strongly religious, but the only kind of worship that appealed to him was the spontaneous variety he had seen among the Africans.

Sir Francis Galton was a scientist and gathered his statistics carefully. Prayer, though, is not so subject to critical analysis. It is the outpouring of a contrite heart, a search by the lonely for fulfillment, the cry of a person who knows that things have gone desperately wrong but doesn't know why:

> *So runs my voice, but what am I?*
> *An infant crying for the light,*
> *An infant crying in the night,*
> *And with no language but a cry.*[5]

---

[5] Lord Tennyson, *In Memoriam.*

Prayer must come from the heart more than the head. John Bunyan said, "When thou prayest, rather let thy heart be without words than thy words be without heart."

IV.

Prayer, too, is more than meditation. In meditation we look within and find the source of strength is oneself. When we pray we go to a source of strength greater than ourselves.

A common mistake in prayer is to try to get God to change his mind, to alter the ordinary course of events to suit our whim. No, prayer cannot change God. Harry Emerson Fosdick said, "God is not a cosmic bell-boy for whom we can press a button to get things." But prayer changes our values and attitudes toward life and love, and opens truth to us. Thus we do not pray for easy lives. We pray to be stronger persons.

James M. Barrie said, "The God to whom little boys say their prayers has a face very like their mother." Fair enough. We learn about love, tenderness, and human affection from the family hearth. That learning remains vital, and religion assures us that something in the very nature of the universe prompts us to beauty, joy, and bonding to other people.

Samuel Taylor Coleridge reminded us how prayer inspires a broader affection:

> He prayeth well, who loveth well
> Both man and bird and beast.
>
> He prayeth best, who lovest best
> All things both great and small;
> For the dear God who loveth us,
> He made and loveth all.[6]

The Bible has many prayers. Jesus prayed on the important occasions

---

[6] *The Rime of the Ancient Mariner.*

in his life: in the Temple, in the Garden of Gethsemane, and on the cross. He told the story of the Pharisee and the publican. We see in that story that the Pharisee did not go to the Temple to pray but to brag. How easily we deceive ourselves. Thus Oscar Wilde commented, "When the gods wish to punish us, they answer our prayers."

When I was in seminary a number of us went daily to morning chapel. It was held at 8:45. Various ministers and professors conducted the 15-minute service. We were seminarians and terribly critical. We thought it was clever to analyze every speaker's style. We tried to determine his theology and particularly what heresy he fell into, all from that brief service.

We found that if you would know a person's real theology, listen to the prayers more than the sermon. It is there that we reveal ourselves. Even if the worship leader reads a prayer by someone else, the fact is that one prayer was chosen instead of another.

Prayer, as James Montgomery said, "is the soul's sincere desire, uttered or unexpressed." Prayer opens a little window to God. Lord Tennyson said, "More things are wrought by prayer than this world dreams of."

Are prayers answered? There is an easy way to tell. If you rise from your prayer a better person, then your prayer was answered. If you pray for wealth, power, and glory, your prayer assuredly will not be answered, or woe betide you if it is. If you pray for wisdom, strength, courage, love, beauty of soul, that prayer most certainly will be answered.

Axioms of Theology

My son, Andrew, majored in mathematics. He did some special work in what then was a new form of math. It was known then as fractal geometry and now is called "chaos." Plane and solid geometry are used to measure areas and solids, but many areas are not simple forms. Fractal geometry was devised to measure shorelines, hilly surfaces, and all kinds of irregular shapes.

We were at a dinner when Andrew explained this to a physicist. The physicist suggested that there is a similarity between pure mathematics and theology in that they both have axioms, and then they develop their theories from those axioms.

My son was interested in that idea. He turned to me and asked if that were so. I said I supposed it was, knowing full well what the next question would be. Predictably, he asked, "What are the axioms of theology?" We then had a long conversation about that important idea.

Axioms, you remember from your study of geometry, are ideas or premises that cannot be proved. They are assumed to be so. For the most part they are obvious: the whole is equal to the sum of its parts, parallel lines will never meet, and so on.

What would the axioms of theology be? As in geometry, we begin with premises that are simple statements of belief. We can judge the value of axioms, in theology as in geometry, by how well they present a meaningful and consistent set of theorems. They must give us a belief system that will hang together, which makes a theology that provides an accurate description of life and the world as we know it.

Each religion will have different axioms. Obviously the fundamentalists use different axioms from the Mormons, who differ from the Roman Catholics, and so on. What axioms do we have?

I.

We speak of religion as a search for truth. Very well, then: what are the truths we find? Let me state some of them briefly and, then let's see what results they provide, what larger truths they point to.

The first axiom is that we can know the truth, at least partly. Some corollaries would be that the truth is worth the commitment it takes to discover it; that knowledge of the truth adds something worthwhile to our lives; that when we know the truth there is a responsibility to live according to the insight it provides.

We could go on with more aspects of that axiom, but you see how it is done. You state a truth and then proceed with its implications. If it's done carefully and without skipping any steps, you arrive at a theology. So the first axiom simply is that *there is truth.*

A second axiom is that there is some purpose in life. We cannot know what that purpose is, certainly not in its entirety. But we can believe that there *is* a purpose. That confidence is necessary. We can then relate our own lives to what we know of life.

That axiom, that there is some purpose in life, is essential. Remember it is an axiom. It cannot be proven. You can, as with Euclidian axioms, change it, and you have a different theology. You can assume there is no purpose, that life is empty and meaningless, and you get a different system. But we assume life is not sham and pretense, that we are not simply results of a cosmic jest. So that is our second axiom: *that there is a purpose in life.*

Our third axiom is that *being human implies duty to others.* We are not alone but meant to live in community and fellowship. We have the duty to attend especially to the least of society, to the

Axioms of Theology

helpless and defenseless. That means we must care for the widow and orphan, the victims of bigotry and violence, the mentally challenged, the physically ill, and those who have known oppression.

That we have duty to other people is so obvious it needs no elaboration. A religion that does not require doing good work is no religion at all. It would deserve our contempt. Nearly as bad is a religion that looks only to its own. We must have compassion toward those denied a stake in contemporary culture by virtue of inadequate education or economic misery.

A fourth axiom in our development of theology is that *we are ruled by a moral law*. As with other axioms, we cannot prove it. We take it as a premise, and it has consequences that make a theology more meaningful in deciding about human nature.

`The moral law simply stated is that there are moral rules that govern the universe. We are here only on condition of good behavior. If we violate those laws we suffer consequences. Use the example of physical laws. Science has discovered many physical laws. Now, scientists do not invent those laws. They describe what already exists. Those laws, such as mechanics, gravity, and other laws of physics, exist whether we know them or not. And you can violate those laws. You can drink poison, jump off a high building, or stick your hand in a fire. But you will pay the consequences. It does not matter what your attitude is or what your intention is. There is a price to be paid for transgression of those laws.

Now, the argument is that there are similar laws in the moral sphere. They are not so easily demonstrated but they can be discerned. The moral laws are fixed, just as the physical laws are, and we do not invent them. They are there whether we know them or not.

How do we discover the moral laws? By observing the human scene. We get help from psychology. We get help from history, from the long tradition of theology, from the ancient mythologies, and from philosophy.

One of the greatest steps forward humanity ever took was in that ancient time when the Ten Commandments were formulated. What is so valuable about the Ten Commandments is not what they specifically say, though they are good rules. What is most important about them is the *concept* of law. In that primitive and fearsome time the world seemed a terrible and frightening place. Earthquakes, floods, eclipses, diseases, frightening animals, all must have thrown terror into people.

Then someone formulated the Ten Commandments. They saw the universe based not just on physical principles but also on moral principles. They perceived that there are some ways that are good, others that are bad. We can know the difference, and as we follow ways that are good, something important is added to our lives.

So there are moral laws. You ask for examples. Well, there are many. For example, a corollary under this axiom would be, *evil is self-inflicted*. I know all the arguments about that, that good things come randomly, not just to those who deserve them, that the evil often prosper while the good suffer hunger and disease. But then you must define what you think is good. If you treasure most of all material things, I suppose the moral law means less. But if you treasure above all else such values as character, self-respect, honesty, generosity, charity, and what we generally call virtue, then you will see that we have treasure in exact proportion as we deserve it, not a whit more or less.

I say that in spite of all the vagaries of existence, most of our evil is self-inflicted, caused by our own vice. You think about it and see how often it is so.

Now, to summarize, we see these four axioms, and we can draw numerous corollaries. The four axioms are:

There is a truth we can know.
There is some purpose in life.
Being human implies duty to others.
We are ruled by a moral law.

II.

Let me suggest two more axioms, and we will have a substantial framework for building a theology.

Axiom five is that we can change the balance of good and evil. What we do makes a difference. Our efforts are not lost in the swirl of time. We can help diminish the awesome sum of evil. We can reduce the amount of hatred by walking the extra mile, by turning the other cheek, by blessing those who curse and revile us, by repaying good for evil.

The future is not set. It unfolds moment by moment and to some extent at least is what we make it. In other words *we control the future by our own goodness.* Take that truth to heart: we control the future by our own goodness. All our suffering, all our good deeds, our heroic sacrifices, make the world better.

We have choices. We can stand aside wringing our hands at the horror of it all, or we can do something about it. Now you may say there is so little we can do. I will not argue whether we have the ability to do much or little. Only am I proposing that we should do what we can. We can smile at the store clerk. We can exchange pleasantries with the mail carrier or help someone who is looking for directions. Every day brings opportunities to be nice to people, to make them feel better about themselves, and to show them we want to be their friends. In the next hour you will have the chance to be nice to someone.

We have love within us that can make someone else's life better. We can have the undying love of the father for his wayward son, the concern of the shepherd who left his 99 sheep to search for the one lost sheep, the devotion of the servant to his trust.

Finally, axiom number six: *there is an intelligent construct to the universe.* As with other axioms, we cannot prove or disprove that statement. But it is sensible and gives a coherent underpinning to what we know of the universe. Why do we say there is an intelligent construct to the universe? Simply because it makes more sense. It provides the best explanation for what we know of life.

We see about us a unified world. After all we speak of a *uni*verse, not a *multi*verse. We believe life is not capricious or accidental. To believe that this complex universe came about as a result of accident is equivalent to believing that an explosion in an electronics factory could produce a computer. We hear that the world after all has its disorderly parts. Planets collide, there are earthquakes, and species disappear. That is so. But on the whole we are impressed with how orderly and dependable nature is.

The study of every science shows us how unbelievably complicated is the world. Physics, chemistry, geology, astronomy—all those disciplines stagger the mind with how complex is the subject they treat. Think how terribly complex is the atom, which has something like 28 different particles in it. Astronomy staggers us with its number of galaxies and stars within each galaxy. And we know from cosmic radiation that the most distant galaxy contains the same elements found here on earth.

It is easier to believe that there is design and intelligence behind all those interweavings, than to believe they are accidental. Now, when we say there is intelligence, immediately we face the question, what is the nature of that intelligence? Ah, there we have our next step, which is a description of God.

III.

This sermon already is long enough and we must stop it somewhere. We could proceed from these axioms to draw a comprehensive theory of God and other facets of religion. We could go on with the doctrine of judgment, doctrines of human nature and immortality. Let me restate the six axioms for you, and you see the beginning of a theology:

Axiom 1: *There is truth that we can know.*
Axiom 2: *There is some purpose in life.*
Axiom 3: *Being human implies duty to others.*
Axiom 4: *We are ruled by a moral law.*
Axiom 5: *We can change the balance of good and evil.*
Axiom 6: *There is an intelligent construct to the universe.*

These constitute religious truths. We could go on to enunciate corollaries and fill in the blanks. Such a method will point us toward the meaning of religion and give substance to our belief that religion is the search for truth. We can also see our involvement in the processes of nature and how we are needed in the whole scheme.

Religion, we believe, is a journey to a promised land. It is paved with the thoughts of great people, with the sweat of those who toiled in the vineyards of the Lord, and with the blood of martyrs who died for our great cause. Let us continue their effort and clasp hands of fellowship as we attempt in our church to search for truth and to erect a visible part of the Kingdom of God here on earth.

The Message of Jesus

*The Spirit of the Lord is upon me, because he has
anointed me to preach good news to the poor.*
—Luke 4.18

Unitarianism began as an attempt to recover the simple Christianity, the pure religion of Jesus, uncluttered by creeds, confessions, and complicated liturgies. Until about 1845, if you asked Unitarians what they believed, they would say, "We believe everything plainly taught in the New Testament and what reasonably can be inferred from it." Then they simplified that to say they believed everything Jesus taught.

What did he teach? What message did he bring that so charmed people who heard him? What message of spiritual nourishment came to those people of the first century, a message so strong that they cast off their former religions, Judaism and Roman paganism, to take the name Christian?

How do we recover Jesus' message? The gospels are the only source. Nothing else credible exists from the first century. And even the New Testament can be hard to sort out. But taking the gospels we can learn much about what Jesus taught.

Jesus began his ministry with the words from Isaiah:

> The Spirit of the Lord is upon me, because he has anointed me to preach good news to the poor.[7]

Before that, John baptized him, and then he was tempted by the Devil for 40 days. Such was the preparation for his call. Jesus went to the synagogue and announced his call with the words of the text. He said God "has anointed me to preach good news to the poor." What is the nature of that "good news"? In short, what is the message of Jesus?

I.

The message of Jesus can be stated briefly thus: his one purpose, a purpose everywhere evident in the gospels, simply, is to teach us about God. Mark wrote,

> Jesus came into Galilee, preaching the gospel of God, and saying, "The time is fulfilled, and the kingdom of God is at hand; repent, and believe in the gospel."[8]

Now, taking the gospels as our sources, we see what are the plain teachings in them. First let us notice what teachings are *not* in them.

Jesus did not intend that anyone should worship him. He did not think himself equal with God or part of a Trinity. He did not speak in hidden or mysterious codes. He spoke openly and then explained when people didn't understand.

Jesus did not intend to overthrow Judaism or set up a new religion. Had anything so revolutionary been on his mind, he would have said so. Any such radical thoughts would require the most urgent appeals. It is obvious that he wanted to reform Judaism. He differed from the Pharisees and the Sadducees, but he

---

[7] Isaiah 61:1.

[8] Mark 1:14–5.

was entirely within the range of normative Judaism. He said he came to fulfill the law, not to abolish it.

As for the Trinity, there is no indication of it anywhere in the gospels. There is not so much as a hint of his belief that he was in any way equal with God. On the contrary, he everywhere showed his subordination to God. Any number of passages comes to mind. "Why do you call me good? There is none good but God alone." He called God "*Our* Father"—yours and mine just as much as his. He said, "You shall worship the Lord your God, and him only shall you serve." His prayers are moving. Do you suppose he prayed to himself? Where, then is that indicated? When he cried on the cross, "My God, my God, why hast thou forsaken me?" do you suppose that last, desperate prayer was a sham? Did he mean something other than the words say? Then it would be incumbent on the writer to tell us what, in fact, was meant, if not the plain meaning of the words. But every circumstance surrounding those words leads us to suppose they were meant just as they were given.

Christianity developed a lot of doctrines that are entirely foreign to the gospels. We have such teachings as the Immaculate Conception, that Mary was conceived without sin, and thus Jesus was born without original sin. There is the doctrine of Mary's ascent directly into heaven. There are doctrines about the dual nature of Christ and his descent into Hell after death. If people want to believe those things, they may do so, but there is no Biblical warrant for them.

II.

The entire intent of Jesus was to teach us about God. He did so with everyday illustrations. He drew on life about him. Think how often he used illustrations from nature. He said foxes have holes and birds have nests, but the Son of Man has not where to lay his head. Jesus said that not a sparrow falls without God's knowledge. He spoke of lilies of the field, which women used as fuel for their ovens, but he saw them arrayed in garments more beautiful than anything Solomon had; yet they neither toil nor spin. God takes care of them.

What does that tell us about God? By those illustrations, he showed God's laws extend to nature as well as to us. He compared the mystery of the coming kingdom to the rising yeast in the flour. God's will is everywhere. God is concerned for all nature, plants, animals, and people. We draw from that the insight that the same laws govern all that exists, all nature.

When Jesus wanted to talk about God's mercy he told the story of a woman who nagged the judge. In the end the judge relented. His point was that if a human judge, with such strict laws to guide him, can be moved to mercy, then how much more will God be merciful to those who plead sincerely.

What else did Jesus tell us about the nature of God? What does God want of us? What is our duty? The priests talked of tithing and obeying laws. Jesus' thoughts turned in another direction. He told the story of a Samaritan. A man was beaten, robbed, and left half dead by the road. A priest and then a Levite came along. They crossed to the other side and pretended not to see him. Then a Samaritan came and stopped to help him. He put the man on his beast, took him to the inn, gave the innkeeper money, told him to look after the unfortunate man, and if there wasn't enough money, he would give him the rest when he returned.

The moral is obvious. The good man is the one who helped the person in need. But in those days it was a radical teaching: that someone from the hated Samaria might be better than people in the religious orders. Jesus, in fact, told three stories about Samaritans, and every time he made the point that they were better than those we usually call religious. Jesus cured ten lepers, and only one took the trouble to thank him. That was the Samaritan. Another time Jesus was thirsty, and only the Samaritan woman gave him water from the well.

He used the same kind of story in talking about human nature and responsibilities. We are like the three kinds of soil: we can be barren, moderately productive, or very productive. We have that choice. We can build faith on a foundation of rock or of sand.

We need to have a sense of what our priorities are, as the man who sold everything to purchase a pearl of great price. We need the devotion of the widow who put her last two coins in the Temple treasury. On the other hand, we ought to avoid the carelessness of the bridesmaids who let all their oil burn and, at the one great hour, had none left.

In other ways Jesus showed what we must avoid. He never criticized anyone for belief or lack of it. He criticized only the single sin of hypocrisy. He railed against those who like to practice their piety in public, that men might see them. Beware, for your Father in Heaven knows all this, he said. God has no use for people who want everyone to know when they give alms, or who like to pray in public, so they will be admired by people. Heaping up empty phrases does no good. It is, in the modern idiom, counterproductive. He scorned the hypocrisy of men who wanted to stone the adulteress while not admitting their own sins.

III.

All right, then. Jesus' message was to teach us about God. He believed there are laws of God that operate through all nature. He believed that there is a unity between people, animals, and plants. All life is joined. There is one God and Father of us all: God not just of people but also of all life. We are all connected. That is the theological basis for the ecological movement.

Jesus believed we could know the will of God, at least partly. What is God's will? That we should be kind to each other, helpful to those who need us, forgiving as we are forgiven. We are to resist temptation. We must use our talents well and develop the fertile soil within. We need an abiding trust in God:

> Be not anxious about your life, what you shall eat or what you shall drink, nor about your body, what you shall put on.[9]

---

[9] Matthew 6:25.

Next we come to miracles. What do we make of them? There are several kinds of miracles. Most deal with healing. In John, Jesus turned water into wine. There are stories about fish and loaves multiplying to feed multitudes. Some stories are vague and may be miracles, such as the Transfiguration, the cursing of the fig tree, and the resurrection. We note this point: that with faith, miraculous things can happen. We don't believe withered hands are restored by faith or that sickness is caused by demons. Yet the point of the miracles is this: *that with sufficient faith many things are possible, even things we might have thought impossible.*

The gospel writers used a literary device we consider unscientific. It isn't fair to expect that they would conform to twentieth-century theories of science. But their point still is valid: that with sufficient faith many things are possible, even things we might have thought impossible. The whole field of psychosomatic medicine shows us how little we understand the relation of the mind and the will to physical well-being. Every physician knows the recovery of a sick person is directly related to the patient's attitude and will to recover.

Jesus saw the importance of faith. The thought is parent to the deed, and we must persuade people to want to do good, to want the well-being of others, to determine themselves to works of mercy and compassion. As you think in your heart, so are you. It is wrong to commit adultery, but it also is wrong to feel lust in your heart. It is wrong to hate, wrong to curse those who ill-use you and who are your enemies.

The life of Jesus, or at least his ministry, was devoted to teaching us about God. He sought to be about his Father's business. And what does that mean, to be about our Father's business? There again, Jesus was clear. The Beatitudes said the blessed ones are the poor in spirit, the meek, those who hunger and thirst after righteousness. Nowhere did Jesus say they are favored who believe the right things, who subscribe to this or that creed, who tithe, recite the right liturgies. On the contrary, "Not every one who says to me, 'Lord, Lord' will enter the Kingdom of Heaven, but he who does the will of my Father which is in heaven."

That point is stressed in Matthew 25. Jesus said those will be saved who gave food to the hungry and drink to the thirsty, welcomed the stranger, clothed the naked, visited the sick, and went to those in prison: "inasmuch as you did it to one of the least of these, my brethren, you did it to me."[10] Is that not clear? Do you sense any hidden meanings? When we ask, "What does the Lord require of you?" the answer becomes plain.

IV.

There is one more quality of God that must be mentioned in this brief listing. It is the love of God. Jesus saw God as a loving force in our lives. When he said, "Our Father," he used the term *abba*. *Abba* is a Hebrew word that means, roughly, "Daddy." It is a familiar term of endearment that one applies to one's own father. Jesus, by the way, is the first one to use the term *abba* for God. It is without any precedent in rabbinic literature.

The parent image is important. It reminds us that we are born into this world in an environment of love and affection. We speak of mother love and the phrase conjures the tenderest associations. The parent image for God is an important one. Our parents may discipline us when we transgress, and sometimes wrongly; but they always love us and will take us back. So is God's love constant. We are not in the world just to drift friendlessly. We are in a universe that enfolds us with caring. We look at the stars and feel a kinship with the world.

Jesus told the story of the prodigal son. The son acted in ways the father disapproved. He rejected his family, but he could not kill the father's love for him. When the son returned, the father welcomed him back. No rebellion of the son could diminish that love: "This, my son, was dead and is alive." Just so, said Jesus, is God's love for us. We make mistakes, deliberate or unintentional. We commit every crime within the province of human imagining. Yet we are never removed from God's mercy.

---

[10] Matthew 25:40.

Theology uses the term "grace." Grace means we are surrounded by love, love not for anything we have done but because of the nature of the universe. So do we call the church the beloved community, a place where we rightly expect to be understood, cared for, and appreciated.

Those are the ideas Jesus gave us about God. Let me list the six major points in his theology—for that is what we are talking about, the theology of Jesus.

First, from the nature stories, we see that people, animals, and all nature are one. The same laws govern and apply to all.

Second, as with the judge who was moved to pity by the woman's pleas, God's mercy is available to all.

Third, as with the parable of the three soils, human nature is open to ever-greater possibilities.

Fourth, the miracle stories teach us the power of faith to change our lives.

Fifth, from the story of the Good Samaritan and the 25th chapter of Matthew, we see that religious duty consists in helping those who need us.

Sixth, from the story of the prodigal son, we learn we are surrounded by love.

Thus we have good insight into the theology of Jesus. There is his central message. He wanted to teach us about God. Churches quarrel over doctrines. They find hidden mysteries that are divisive. But those have nothing to do with what Jesus taught. You see, there never has been dispute over the Golden Rule, the Beatitudes, or the message of love.

Finally, why do we learn about God from Jesus? He was so God-like that in him people saw a reflection of the deity. "Come, follow me," he said and by that they understood that they too possessed a spirit of the divine. We have those God-like qualities in us, too. We need only open ourselves to that high calling to realize the greatness that is humanity at its best.

Unitarians have always said we believe in the religion *of* Jesus rather than the religion *about* Jesus. That is our standard. Let us strive to be the best we are and might be. Jesus says to us, let us open ourselves to the possibilities that in our best moments we are: merciful, loving, generous, compassionate. So we can become Emmanuel: God with us. There is a resource of great inspiration waiting for us, and it is ours as soon as we will give ourselves over to those finer impulses that lie in the conscience, for there is the living God, really and truly. That is what Jesus was telling people. That is his message.

Religious Experience

*"Be thou to me a rock of refuge, a strong fortress,
to save me, for thou art my rock and my fortress."*
—Psalm 71:3

God often is spoken of as a rock. In that is implied dependability, firmness, something that does not bend in the wind or wash away with the rains.
So the Psalmist said,

> To thee, O Lord, I call;
> my rock, be not deaf to me.[11]

Moses said to the Jews in the wilderness, in his prayer, "The Rock, his work is perfect; for all his ways are justice."[12]

Jesus, describing the religious person, used the image of a man who built his house on a foundation of rock. Thus if we rely on God we have a faith that will weather the trials of life, that will not abandon us in our grief or despair.

---

[11] Psalm 28:11.

[12] Deuteronomy 32:4.

The Price of Truth

I.

What, then, is religion? It is belief, how you see the universe, how you view your relation to other people. Religion is learning, and in our schools and colleges we teach people what others have said. The wisdom of the past has much that can benefit us.

Religion, though, must be got first-hand. It must be experienced. Sometimes people *study* religion and think that is religion. It isn't. It's one thing to know about religion, another to feel it. Religion is not just belief. It is not just ethics or duty. It is more than knowledge. Those things are needed. They are so obvious, they require no further convincing. But they are not religion.

Religion is experience. Indeed, sometimes religion may leave us while we discuss it. I study religion much of the time; but it can be overstudied, too. Books show us only the shadow of religion, the ghosts of faith. Neither theological colleges nor historic cathedrals, neither logic nor Gothic architecture can give us more than the ghost of religion. Carl Jung said that, for many people, religion is a substitute for religious experience. It is an interesting distinction.

Now, this idea of religious experience needs to be qualified immediately. When we speak of experience, we are apt to call to mind the mystics and saints. William James wrote a great work called *The Varieties of Religious Experience*. James wrote a valuable book. But see: he took religious experience and *studied* it. Others can read the book and think, "But I have had no such experience; therefore I am not truly religious." We read of the mystic experiences of St. Paul or Thomas Aquinas and we think, "I am not like them, so I must not be religious."

I heard a crude expression of that idea. A fundamentalist said to me, "You don't need to study all those books. Just let Jesus into your life." Maybe you've heard that, too. As much as we might regret siding with a fundamentalist, he pointed to the idea that religion begins as experience and must remain so. Sometimes we liberals in theology are too far toward the rational. We reject what we can't understand. If we can't see, touch, feel, taste, or smell it, then it must not be so.

RELIGIOUS EXPERIENCE

Sir James Fraser in *The Golden Bough* wrote about how early human beings felt that life was bound up with nature. They saw that the same processes that freeze the stream and strip the earth of vegetation might also portend human extinction. Later people imagined that the means of averting calamity were in their own hands—at first by magic incantations and spells and later through science and technology. Yet hurricanes and earthquakes remind us that we are subjects of nature, not masters. The whole environmental movement tells us that we play fast and loose with nature at our peril, that our despoliation of the earth will cause our own doom.

What those ancients sensed has returned to us with urgency. We see that our science has deluded us. The earth is not our toy. We cannot go on creating ever greater bombs, eliminating more species, wasting the earth's resources. There is a price to be paid. As the common saying has it, "There's no free lunch." What we take, we must pay for.

So we learn that there are deeper causes, some mightier power, behind the shifting scenes of history.

II.

We must not at all discount the importance of critical study. There have been some questionable consequences, though. The scientific study of religion has not done much, as far as I know, to bring religious experience to those who had none before or to deepen it in those who had it already. It may have done a disservice by giving the impression that religious experience is the province of a small minority of the human race. We must not think of genuine religion as belonging to those with highly disciplined or educated minds, or to those who have had strange and unusual experiences of God. There has grown up, because of all this literature on mysticism, a feeling that a few have religious experience, but the majority does not.

I have read some books on the mystics. I have had no such conversion experience as St. Augustine. I have not the great mind of

Martin Buber, and I have not the sacrificial devotion of Albert Schweitzer.

What do you conclude, then, if that is true of you? That you are weak in your faith? That light comes to others, which has not come to you? That God is revealed to only a few, not including us? Have we then committed a sin against the Holy Ghost? Is something wrong with our souls?

So the urgings toward religion usually made by preachers and evangelists can be discouraging for us ordinary people. We do not have such religious experiences or even dedication like that of the mystics and saints. We are apt to conclude, then, that we are not religious, that we are not among the privileged souls.

I want to make clear the point: that we, all of us, do have religious experiences, but our learning sometimes causes us not to recognize it. We do not have to be mystics or be born again or have degrees in philosophy.

III.

William Blake wrote,

> *To see a World in a Grain of Sand*
> *And a Heaven in a Wild Flower,*
> *Hold Infinity in the palm of your hand*
> *And eternity in an hour.*
> *Eternity, God, religion, beauty, joy:*
> *they are there all the time.*

Wordsworth wrote,

> *My heart leaps up when I behold*
> *A rainbow in the sky.*

The beauty is not in the rainbow but in my response to the heavens. Joy, goodness, love, all the fruits of religion are within us all the time. It is like the story that Maurice Maeterlinck wrote about the bluebird: a boy searched everywhere for the bluebird and at last found it in his own back yard.

I want you to broaden your idea of religious experience. Nor do I mean only beauty and loveliness. Sadness and grief, too, bring understanding. The Psalmist wrote,

> Come, behold the works of the Lord,
> How he has wrought desolation in the earth.[13]

Is God not experienced in defeat and frustration? Jesus found God in his confrontation with Satan in the wilderness. Do we not in our extremities of grief and sadness encounter a Power that reminds us of the majesty of God? And do we not, with age, gain the confidence that if we could only see beyond our knowledge we would trust the workings of the creative forces of the universe? When we have bested tragedy, when we have withstood torment, denial, betrayal, and grief, then we sense that there is that in the universe which moves toward the higher good. We gain confidence that we are part of something great and enduring, confidence that we are not stranded in a cold, friendless world.

We are distracted away from those ideas. Real religion is to experience the holy in our lives, not just in the occasional, cataclysmic events, but also in life as it comes to us day by day. Tennyson saw God in the "flower in the crannied wall" and said that if we could truly understand that flower, we would know all there is to know. Why would you look for God in the earthquake, the fire, the flood, and the wind, when God is in the still, small voice? Would you go to the mountaintop, when you need only look about you at the mockingbird, the clouds, and the wild flowers? Why study lives of the saints when God is truly in your friends, in every person you meet, and inside you? Epictetus wrote, "You carry God about with you, you poor wretch, and know it not."

God is found in every human encounter. In the wedding

---

[13] Psalm 46:8.

service there is a third party present; and in the funeral God watches with the same care that nourished the person through life.

L. P. Jacks told this story. He met one of the great school masters and asked him, "Where in your time-table do you teach religion?" "We teach it all day long," he answered. "We teach it in arithmetic, by accuracy. We teach it in language, by learning to say what we mean—'yea, yea and nay, nay!' We teach it in history, by humanity. We teach it in geography, by breadth of mind. We teach it in handicraft, by thoroughness. We teach it in astronomy, by reverence. We teach it in the playground, by fair play. We teach it in kindness to animals, by courtesy to servants, by good manners to one another, and by truthfulness in all things. We teach it by showing the children that we, their elders, are their friends and not their enemies."

"But what," asked Prof. Jacks, "about the different denominations? Have you no trouble with the parents?" "None at all," he replied. And he concluded, "I do not want religion brought into this school from the outside. What we have of it, we grow ourselves."

You, too: you do not need religion brought into you from the outside. Grow it yourself. That was the method of Jesus. He said to the Pharisees, "I say you are gods, sons of the Most High, every one of you." Jesus saw God in the faith of the Samaritan, in the Syro-Phoenician woman at the well, in the humility of the Publican, the diligence of the man searching for the pearl of great price, the forgiveness of the father for his wayward son, the joy of the shepherd who found his lost sheep.

God lives within you: really and truly lives within you. Are you shocked when you see starving children shown on the television, when you read of the slaughter in Northern Ireland, or read of the street people? Are you touched at the heartache, grief, and sorrow of people all over the earth? What, then, is the source of that shock and pain you feel? Is it not a higher source entering your heart?

I speak here of the common experience, not the rare mystical one. You feel tenderness watching animals and their young, seeing a child at play, or watching the stars and clouds. You experience beauty in the flowers and lakes and sheep in the fields. Whence comes that tenderness? Whence comes the love you feel toward those close to you? "The heavens declare the glory of God," said the Psalmist.

You feel within you such emotions as justice, courage, the urge to reach toward those who need help, the desire to right wrongs, to share your crust with the hungry. You also feel the urge to share your love, to bind your heart to another.

Those things are the experience of religion. At all those times God is found in the human heart. The Spirit of the Living God does not await your recognition at the critical moments or the peak experiences that come but rarely. God is there all the time.

Prayers

Used in Worship at
Emerson Unitarian Church

The Price of Truth

Let us pray. O God, grant us a vision of thy city in all its splendor: a city of justice, where none shall prey on others; a city of plenty, where vice and poverty shall cease to fester; a city of love where all success shall be founded on service and honor shall be given to nobleness alone; a city of peace, where order shall not rest of force but on the love of all for the city, the great mother of the common life and weal. Hear thou, O Lord, the prayer of all our hearts as we each pledge our time and strength and thought so to speed the day of her coming beauty and righteousness.

Bind us in one spirit with all humankind through our prayers and our labors, that occasions of strife may be lessened and that counsels of selfishness may be turned into concern for the common good.

O God, our true life, who through thy will dost guide our actions and thoughts, help us in our struggle on the upward path. Help us to find the joy and happiness that can come from serving thee. *Amen.*

Let us pray. Creator of all, fill us more and more with the sense of mutual support. Give us a conviction of purpose to life, that we may respond more readily to its demands. Let sincerity, good will, and filial trust encompass us. So many things about us and within us are disheartening. So often are we disappointed in others and in ourselves, and we cry out against nature. Convince us, Spirit of Truth, of thy presence even in the utmost extremity of misery and wrong. Show us how the weak may become heroic, and the simple be filled with understanding, and the erring retrace their ways.

Out of the confusions of human passion, lead us, O God, into order and peace. May we go forward without fear along the paths of justice, helping to open new approaches to truth and good. And may the spirit that was in Jesus dwell in our hearts also, sustaining us in our efforts and assuring us that no endeavors after righteousness are lost. *Amen.*

Let us pray. O Lord of Life, we come here with the hope of doing better than we did yesterday, and to find strength to proceed on the path of duty. Yet we would ask that religion not be too somber, but that duty be touched with delight, and that we find our journey together accompanied by the thrill of adventure and accomplishment.

May the bustle of this busy city not distract us from seeing the small things that count: lending a hand to help someone, speaking words of kindness and appreciation to those who are around us, and spreading such joy as opportunity presents. May we not wait for great and noble causes, but seek the ordinary tasks that call for signs of love and affection. May we do what we can to erase the sorrow and pain of the world, and eliminate the hiding-places of hatred. May the material things we have be turned into means of grace and joy. Let our spirits be refreshed here, as we drink from the cup of a holy communion with thee and with each other. May our spirits be strengthened in the wise to make our church a holy place, where all good thoughts are welcome, and nothing be banished but that which is hateful in thy sight. *Amen.*

Let us pray. Spirit Divine, help us to see the wonders of thy creation, and the boundless goodness that exists about us. May we, in all our relations with each other, strive toward the spread of love and kindness, so that we make not only our own lives but also the lives of all others the richer.

May we also, O God, learn to approach life with humility. Make us never so insecure that we fail to admit our own weaknesses. Strengthen us so that we stand, yes; but also teach us to fall: to fall from the heights of glory we build about ourselves, to fall from the vain sense of pride that makes us sometimes foolish, sometimes haughty.

Give us strength to rise to the full heights of humanity; but also weaken us when we are hostile, when we are angry at one another, when suspicions crowd out our better instincts. Give us a purer faith: not faith that tells us we are better than others, or which blinds us to our faults, but faith that will open our eyes to a gentler being, a nobler sympathy, a deeper awareness of our common tasks. So may we march together, hand in hand, toward that kingdom which, partly through our efforts, we may achieve. *Amen.*

Let us pray. Creator Spirit, who hast in mercy taught us how good it is to follow the holy desires in our hearts, and how bitter is the grief of falling short of what beauty our minds behold, strengthen us to walk steadfastly through life in the better path we know should be ours. Give us wisdom to tread it prudently as well as cheerfully; so that we may rest secure in the knowledge that we have done our best.

May our hearts be filled with good and righteous desires. May the longing of our souls not be satisfied until we have labored diligently in the cause of righteousness. Open our minds to the counsels of eternal wisdom. Breathe into our souls the peace that passes understanding. Let our hunger and thirst for justice be filled. May we seek thy kingdom, O God, and may our hearts be thy dwelling place. Let us go forth with the light of hope in our eyes and the fire of inspiration in our lives. With love in our hearts, may we do thy will, this day and forever more. *Amen.*

Let us pray. Almighty and eternal Spirit of Truth, grant unto us thy most precious gifts: strength, wisdom, and courage. Give us wisdom to know thy will, courage to accept it, and strength to carry it out. And grant us the grace to see the precious gifts bestowed on us. Help us to know that true happiness comes when we forget ourselves in the higher service of humanity, and so come closer to thee. May we find thy face, O God, not so much in the heavens as in the countenances of other people, and especially the people who sorrow, who walk a lonely path, and who persevere in faith that sometimes makes hard demands on them.

May we find thy face reflected in the spirits of those who love. May we be strong enough to help each other. And accept, O God, our doubts and anxieties. If we are not certain, make our uncertainty a source of strength. Help us to receive well the heritage given us by the prophets and seers, and may we be worthy to be called thy disciples. *Amen.*

Let us pray. Here may the spirit of beauty and goodness take us into new worlds of service. May we become servants of the greater good and masters of none. Let us find here, in our worship, an ever-flowing fount of inspiration.

O God, comfort the bereaved among us and allay their fears. Thou who art always more ready to give than we to receive, take from us our inclinations toward evil. If we are selfish, it is only because we are weak. If we are cruel, it is because our knowledge is imperfect. If we fail in so many ways, it is because we do not know what we do.

O God, we are inheritors of the good of those who have gone before. Grant that we may be worthy successors to that mighty heritage. May we never forsake it. May that truth that shall make us free dwell in our hearts. May we be living testimony to the truth to which we are witness. May we cease to defend our religion, and learn to practice it. *Amen.*

Let us pray. We come today to find strength and to put our lives in better order. We seek to know the path we should tread, and how to conduct our lives so that each person we know shall be influenced by the love we bear.

Help us, O God, to contain our less worthy desires and to find some answer to our problems. In times of trial and sorrow, may we be patient and humble. Let us worship with open hearts and with firm resolve to do what is right. Let our defeats and grief bring us new determination. May happiness and sorrow, each coming to us in turn, not dissuade us from going to deeper faith. And when we do not understand, then let our trust be all the stronger.

So may every act of kindness and every deed of mercy light the path we travel. And hear, then, the silent promptings of each heart. *Amen.*

Let us pray. Infinite Spirit, creator of all good things and giver of all beautiful things, be with us in our times of need. Let us find thee within the human soul, and so realize peace and happiness, joy and contentment. Be to us as cool waters to quench our thirst for truth. Be to us the living fire of inspiration, and as the evening breeze that stimulates our faith.

May we not doubt that we are part of something majestic and great in the universe. Help us to know that there is a purpose, even when the dark clouds of despair cause us to lose sight of the goodness surrounding us. May we have faith that we shall, in good time, overcome the struggles of existence. While we know not what lies ahead, nor the meaning of what has passed, let us still trust that everything leads to good, and that nothing happens in vain. *Amen.*

Prayer for the New Year

Let us pray. O God, as we finish another year and turn our thoughts to the coming days, grant us inward peace. Let our hearts be at rest, free from the encumbrances of sin, free from the guilt of wrongs we have committed, free from the terrible burden of hate and anger that so often reared itself within us.

Give us the power to increase the store of happiness in the world. May we do our part in bringing thy kingdom even a little closer, and narrow the distance between earth and heaven. Let us spread the healing balm of comfort to those who mourn. Let us be companion to those who are alone. Let us cheer the depressed and show those who see the years slipping by too quickly that they remain in thy care.

May the New Year give us new challenges, and also the strength to meet them. Let the coming year be a new day for our spirits, which so often have been tired. O God, may thy bounteous goodness nourish us and thy mercy be with us through all our days. *Amen.*

Easter Prayer

Let us pray. Divine Spirit, on this holy day we commemorate the rebirth of hope, the triumph of Jesus over all his enemies could do to destroy him. It is the rebirth of hope within every breast, and may we know that this is the promise given to us all: that evil will endure for a moment, but good is forever. May we know that Thou wilt not forsake us nor leave us in our despair; that there is in each of us a spirit that reflects thy light and thy beauty.

May we know that within and about us are resources that will protect us from final destruction. May the love we have for those now dead persuade us that they are a living presence, that immortality is certain to such as hold within their hearts the ideals and dreams that will build the promised kingdom.

O may all, people of every persuasion, of very color and every station in life, know that our cries are not in vain, and that thou art with us through all the travail and anguish that is our lot. *Amen.*

Thanksgiving Prayer

Let us pray. Heavenly Spirit, on this Thanksgiving we remember those things we possess, but we also would think about the blessings we still desire. We are grateful for the gift of friends who sustain us in time of need. We thank thee for giving us work, that our labors might not be in vain. We thank thee for every source of strength, for the love of family, and for the precious heritage of freedom that is ours.

But we would ask, O God, for more blessings than those. Give unto us the ability to see the goal and the result of our strivings. Save us from the confusion of our times and let eternal harmony descend on us. We ask for faith when we cannot see the reason for our trembling hearts. For those who are weak, we ask strength. Send sympathy to the lonely, trust to those who are unsure. We ask, too, for the speedy coming of the day when all who seek after righteousness shall strive together, that the divisions among us shall disappear. So may our lives be set in perfect harmony, and thy kingdom come on earth, as it is in heaven. *Amen.*

Christmas Prayer

Let us pray. O thou creator of all life, and who hast called for us a brother, and for thyself a son, let this season usher in a new kingdom in the hearts of men and women. Send forth thy spirit speedily into the dark places of our sorrow and fear, even as long ago thou didst bring holiness into the stable. May this season bring to an end all oppression. May greed and arrogance, pride and lust, and every false idol of the soul be banished.

May the spirit of Christmas bring hope to the fearful, strength to the weak, and faith to those who mourn. Let strife and tumult be stilled, and in their place the knowledge of thy love cover the earth. May the spirit that was in Jesus be in us also, and let our hearts be taken captive by thy joy, and our minds realize the heavenly powers that have been given to us all. *Amen.*

Prayer for the Country

Let us pray. O Lord, look with favor on our country and give us the wisdom to maintain its cherished ideals. May we grasp again the vision that guided the founders from a foreign shore to seek wider room for their souls.

We ask for thy guidance especially on those who lead: the President and his envoys, that they may govern wisely. We ask guidance for those who write our laws, that they may work selflessly for the welfare of us all. Hear our prayers that peace will continue throughout the land, that strife and dissension will be no more, and the healing balm of thy grace spread over all the people.

May we not shirk the duty to which we are summoned. Help us that we think not of selfish goals, but of the larger good. So may we bequeath to those who follow the legacy given us, that freedom may find its fortress here. *Amen.*

I wish for the dull a little understanding, and for the understanding a little poetry. I wish a heart for the rich and a little bread for the poor. I wish some love for the lonely and some comfort for the grieved.

I wish companionship for those who must spend their evenings alone. I wish contentment for the aged, who see the days slipping by too quickly, and I wish dreams for the young. I wish strength for the weak and courage for those who have lost their faith. And I wish we might all be a little kinder to each other.

Benediction

The love of God hallow every home and every heart; the light of truth ever shine bright before you, and bless you with wisdom, strength, and peace. *Amen.*

www.ingramcontent.com/pod-product-compliance
Lightning Source LLC
Chambersburg PA
CBHW031255290426
44109CB00012B/591